Contents

W9-BFS-929

Author

JoAnn Cairns became a Christian in her early teens through the ministry of The Salvation Army. She graduated from Asbury College with a major in chemistry and worked as a research chemist for a number of years.

Gradually realizing that her heart lay in Christian ministry, particularly in Bible teaching, JoAnn earned a master's degree in Christian education at Wheaton College. For several years she taught courses in Bible study methods at the college and graduate school. She continues to teach a Bible class, and speaks to women's groups.

JoAnn is also the author of *God's Plan for the World* (1982), *God's Plan for Me* (1983), *Faith—Greater Expectations* (1983), and *Welcome Stranger; Welcome Friend* (1988).

SAINTS SINNERS AND A SOVEREIGN GOD

A NEW LOOK AT THE OLD TESTAMENT
A BIBLE STUDY BY JOANN CAIRNS

NAVPRESS

A MINISTRY OF THE NAVIGATORS
P.O. BOX 6000, COLORADO SPRINGS, COLORADO 80934

The Navigators is an international Christian organization. Jesus Christ gave His followers the Great Commission to go and make disciples (Matthew 28:19). The aim of The Navigators is to help fulfill that commission by multiplying laborers for Christ in every nation.

NavPress is the publishing ministry of The Navigators. NavPress publications are tools to help Christians grow. Although publications alone cannot make disciples or change lives, they can help believers learn biblical discipleship, and apply what they learn to their lives and ministries.

COVER ART:
1. *The Archangel Gabriel*; MASOLINO da Panicale; National Gallery of Art, Washington; Samuel H. Kress Collection.
2. *Moses Breaking the Tables of Law*; Gustave DORE.
3. *Engraving of Lamb*; GILBERT.
4. *The Finding of Moses*; Sebastien BOURDON; National Gallery of Art, Washington; Samuel H. Kress Collection.

Scripture quotations in this publication are from the *Holy Bible: New International Version* (NIV). Copyright © 1973, 1978, 1984, International Bible Society. Used by permission of Zondervan Bible Publishers.

Printed in the United States of America

FOR A FREE CATALOG OF
NAVPRESS BOOKS & BIBLE STUDIES,
CALL TOLL FREE 800-366-7788 (USA)
or 800-263-2664 (CANADA)

To Ben

Before You Begin

"It's dull."

"It's boring."

"The people are primitive and outdated."

"It's just a lot of names, places, and dates."

"I get so tired of all of those kings."

"So much of what happens seems unfair."

If these statements express your idea of an Old Testament overview, this study is not for you, for the Old Testament is much more than lists of names, battles, and kings. As we study its record, we see an absolutely holy God revealing Himself to a sinful, undeserving race and to sinful, undeserving individuals. We are awed by His transcendence. We are amazed by the complexity of His workings as He intervenes in the powers of the world, and even nature, to accomplish His purpose.

When we think about circumstances from the perspective of the men and women of the Old Testament, the characters spring to life. We are challenged by the faith of men who laid their lives on the line to be true to God. We are shamed by the examples of people who exhibited the same weaknesses and failures that we see in ourselves. The servants of God become models for us in times of difficulty or challenge. Most of all, we come to know the God of the Old Testament in a more vital, intimate way. None of us can seriously study those books without seeing our lives changed and renewed.

Each of the twenty-four lessons in this study is divided into five subdivisions. You may choose either to complete one subdivision a day or to to complete the entire study at one sitting.

Each lesson also includes charts designed to assist you in organizing the information in a manner that will facilitate an understanding of the patterns of human behavior and of God's activities. Many of these charts include sample responses, which are set in italic type.

Occasionally the study contains questions in which you are asked to mentally place yourself in the position of one of the Old Testament characters, either real or fictional. You may be asked to write a newspaper article, for example. Bonus questions are optional, but are included to give you further opportunity to use your creativity and, in the process, help you to understand the people and events better.

Undoubtedly, questions will come to mind as you complete these lessons. These questions may relate to the meaning of the biblical text or to its application in your life. If the answer to such a question is not immediately apparent, record that question at the end of the lesson under the heading "Your Questions." After completing a lesson, review the questions in the lesson and your responses, looking for answers to the questions you wrote down. If those questions are still unresolved, you may want to discuss them with another person who is involved in Bible study. If you are part of a group study, you will have opportunity to discuss those questions during the group discussion.

The only materials necessary for the completion of these lessons are a Bible and pen. However, you may find the following helpful:

1) A concordance. You may have one in your Bible or you may want to consider a complete concordance, such as *Cruden's, Young's,* or *Strong's.*

2) A Bible atlas or set of maps. The following two works are relatively inexpensive and are very helpful in studying the travels of individuals or groups and the settings of various events: a) Harry Thomas Frank, ed. *Atlas of the Bible Lands.* Maplewood, New Jersey: Hammond Inc. b) Simon Jenkins. *Bible Mapbook.* Belleville, Michigan: Lion Publishing Corporation.

3) A Bible dictionary. A good example is: Merrill C. Tenney, ed. *Zondervan Pictorial Bible Dictionary.* Grand Rapids: Zondervan Publishing House. A Bible dictionary is particularly helpful when you are uncertain of the identity of an individual, place, or practice named in the scriptural account.

4) A commentary such as John F. Walvoord and Roy B. Zuck, eds. *The Bible Knowledge Commentary.* Wheaton: Victor Books. You will often find answers to questions in commentaries, but it is important that you do not let a commentary take the place of studying the Scripture.

5) A Bible handbook. One example is: Merrill F. Unger. *The New Unger's Bible Handbook.* Chicago: Moody Press. Here you will find summaries of Scripture passages and background information to supplement the biblical content.

6) V. Gilbert Beers. *The Victor Handbook of Bible Knowledge.* Wheaton: Victor Books. This work takes selected events from biblical history and combines them with a synopsis of the setting and the cultural and historical background information.

These lessons have been written to facilitate your understanding of God as you see Him at work in the lives of men and women and in the events of a sinful world. May you experience the truth that the events and truths recorded in the Old Testament were "written to teach us, so that through endurance and the encouragement of the Scriptures we might have hope" (Romans 15:4).

What Is Wrong with Our World?

Genesis 1-11

The first eleven chapters of Genesis cover thousands, or even billions or trillions, of years. Only a few carefully selected events from that time are recorded for us. Yet these eleven chapters answer important questions, such as:

How did our world come into being?
How did life begin?
If God created a perfect world, why did He allow it to become so wicked?
How does God deal with sinful humanity?
Why are human beings so unsuccessful in building a peaceful and perfect world?

DAY 1

The beginning of the world as we know it is described in the first two chapters of Genesis.

1. Read the chronological account of the Creation in Genesis 1 and note what God created each day.

SCRIPTURE	DAY	CREATION
Genesis 1:3-5	*1*	*Light and darkness*
Genesis 1:6-8		
Genesis 1:9-13		

SCRIPTURE	DAY	CREATION
Genesis 1:14-19		
Genesis 1:20-23		
Genesis 1:24-31		

2. a. How does the Bible describe the world before the Creation (Genesis 1:2; 2:4-5) and after the Creation (Genesis 2:8-14)?

Before

After

b. How did God describe His own work (Genesis 1:31)?

c. How did God respond after completing His work (Genesis 2:1-3)?

DAY 2

3. Read the account of the creation of Adam and Eve in Genesis 1:26-30, 2:7, and 2:20-25.

a. What model did God use for creating mankind?

b. What raw material(s) did God use in creating

Adam?

10

Eve?

c. Why did God create Eve?

d. What responsibilities did God assign to Adam and Eve?

e. What restrictions did God place upon Adam and Eve (Genesis 2:15-17)?

f. Based on your responses to questions 3a-e,

in what ways were Adam and Eve alike?

in what ways were Adam and Eve different?

---

4. Read Genesis 1:1-2:14 again and list adjectives (at least four) to describe God's creation.

---

5. God placed Adam and Eve in a perfect environment without sin, in the Garden of Eden. We are not told how long they lived in the garden—it may have been a few hours or billions of years. They might have remained there forever, but the events of Genesis 3 changed their future and affect us today. Read Genesis 3 and answer the following questions:

a. What major event is described?

b. What consequences followed that event?

6. a. What did the serpent imply about God in Genesis 3:1-5?

   b. What might we discover about Eve and her allegiance to God from her response to the serpent (Genesis 3:2-6)?

   c. What do we find out about Adam and his allegiance to God from his response to Eve (Genesis 3:6)?

   d. How was life different for Adam and Eve after eating the fruit (Genesis 3:7-11)?

7. Answer the questions listed below for one of the following:

   the serpent (Genesis 3:14-15)
   Eve (Genesis 3:16)
   Adam (Genesis 3:17)
   Adam and Eve (Genesis 3:21-24)

   a. How did God punish the individual?

   b. In what ways was the person's life different because of God's punishment?

   c. How did God's punishment change the person's relationship with others?

BONUS QUESTION

Imagine that you are a news reporter assigned to cover the events of Genesis 3. Select one of the above characters to interview. Using the Scripture passage given above and your own imagination, write a brief report on your interview. Your report should contain the facts from the perspective of the character interviewed.

DAY 4

8. Genesis 3-11 contains a repeated pattern of human sin and God's judgment. Read the appropriate Scriptures and complete the following chart:

TYPE OF SIN	PERSONS GUILTY	EFFECT ON OTHERS	GOD'S RESPONSE
Genesis 3:1-24 *Disbelieving God's Word; disobeying God's command*	*Adam and Eve*	*Every person born a sinner.*	*Banished Adam and Eve from garden. Promised a Savior.*
Genesis 4:1-16 *Envy, hatred*			
Genesis 6:5-7:24 *Evil thoughts*			

TYPE OF SIN	PERSONS GUILTY	EFFECT ON OTHERS	GOD'S RESPONSE
Genesis 11:1-9 *Refusing to acknowledge God*			

DAY 5

9. It is easy for us to look at the sins recorded in Genesis 3-11 and decide that they are from a bygone era. But these sins are present today. Think of one present-day example of each type of sin. Be specific. For example, shoplifting and income tax evasion are examples of disobeying God's command not to steal.

Disbelieving God's Word

Disobeying God's command

Envy

Hatred

Evil thoughts

Failure to acknowledge God

10. Look at your chart in question 8. How did God consistently respond to sin?

11. Read Romans 3:10, 3:23, 5:8, 6:23, and 8:1 to answer the following questions:

a. Who is guilty of sin today?

14

b. How does God respond to sin?

c. What has God provided for those who sin?

d. How have you responded to His provision?

YOUR QUESTIONS

What Is a Life of Faith?

Genesis 11:27-28:20

Thousands of years are recorded for us in Genesis 1-11. After the Fall, God particularly blessed the men and women who obeyed Him. The last part of chapter 11 introduces us to Abram (hereafter referred to as Abraham). God singled out Abraham and his offspring from among the rest of the human race for His particular blessing. From that point until New Testament times, people were required to become Israelites in order to relate to God.

DAY 1

1. Read Genesis 11:27-12:9 and Joshua 24:2 and answer the following questions about Abraham's background:

   a. Where did he grow up?

   b. What god(s) did his father worship?

   c. Why did Abraham leave the city of his childhood?

   d. Why do you think God chose him?

2. Read Genesis 12-23 quickly (you may want to use a modern paraphrase). As you read, write down your impressions of Abraham.

DAYS 2 and 3

3. From Genesis 12:2-3, Genesis 15:5, and Genesis 15:18, make a list of all that God promised Abraham.

4. In future generations, the entire nation looked to Abraham as a spiritual model. He was cited as an example of faith in action (James 2:21-24, Hebrews 11:8-12) and was known as God's friend (James 2:23), but what kind of person was he? One way we can learn about him is to study his actions.

   Complete the chart on this page. Read the Scripture passages and briefly summarize what Abraham did in the column headed "Actions." In the column headed "Character," list basic character traits, such as honesty, selfishness, and loyalty. In the column headed "Values," list actions, people, or possessions that Abraham considered important. (Some spaces may be left blank.)

ACTION	CHARACTER	VALUES
Genesis 12:10-20 *Fearful for his life, he said Sarah was his sister, not his wife.*	*Cowardly*	*His own life*
Genesis 13:5-9 *Gave Lot the choice of the land*	*Unselfishness*	*God's promise of the land*
Genesis 14:1-16		

18

ACTION	CHARACTER	VALUES
Genesis 14:18-20		
Genesis 16:1-6		
Genesis 18:1-8		
Genesis 18:16-33		
Genesis 20:1-13		

5. a. Abraham is characterized as an example of faith. As you think of his life, what events seem inconsistent with a life of faith?

b. How can this encourage you and me?

DAY 4

6. a. Review your answers to questions 1-5. In what ways did Abraham exemplify faith and obedience?

19

b. What additional insights into Abraham's character do we find in Hebrews 11:8-19?

DAY 5

7. Abraham's nephew, Lot, accompanied him to Canaan. Describe Abraham's relationship with Lot, based on the following passages:

Genesis 12:4-5

Genesis 13:1-18

Genesis 14:1-16

Genesis 18:16-33

8. a. From your study of the life of Abraham, list several (at least four) suggestions for a person wanting to live a life of faith.

b. Which of these suggestions seem appropriate for you to develop in your own life?

c. Considering the above suggestions, what specific action will you take to begin developing a life of faith?

YOUR QUESTIONS

How Can I Exemplify Faith?

Genesis 24-32

Abraham had two sons: Ishmael and Isaac. God said that He would fulfill His promise to Abraham through Isaac, the younger of the two. Isaac also had two sons: Esau and Jacob. Again, God chose to fulfill His promises through the younger son, Jacob. These men, like their father, Abraham, are examples of faith for us. Through the line of Isaac and Jacob, the nation of Israel emerged, and God, in His time, sent His Son into the world.

DAY 1

1. a. Compare the promises God made to Abraham, to Isaac, and to Jacob.[1]

PERSON	SCRIPTURE	PROMISE(S)
Abraham	Genesis 12:2-3	
	Genesis 15:4-5	
	Genesis 15:18	
Isaac	Genesis 26:3-4	
Jacob	Genesis 28:13-15	

b. Underline the promises that God made to all three men.

DAY 2

2. Read the account of the search for the right wife for Isaac in Genesis 24.

   a. Describe Abraham's standards for Isaac's wife (verses 3-4).

   b. How did Abraham's requirements reveal his faith in God?

   c. What do we discover about Rebekah?

      Genesis 24:15

      Genesis 24:16

      Genesis 24:18-20

      Genesis 24:24-25

      Genesis 24:58

3. What do we learn about Isaac from each of the following passages?

   Genesis 25:21

   Genesis 25:28

   Genesis 26:1-6

Genesis 26:7-11

Genesis 26:12-24

DAY 3

---

4. Read the adventures of Jacob in Genesis 25:19-35, 26:27-33:20, and 35:1-5. Read quickly, looking for main events rather than details.

   a. If you had to choose a person suited for God's use, for what characteristics would you look?

   b. How is Jacob's character consistent with your expectations?

   c. In what ways does Jacob fail to meet your expectations of a person God will use?

DAY 4

---

5. The name *Jacob* means "he deceives." How did Jacob live up to his name in each of the following situations?

   Genesis 27:1-36

6. Jacob experienced two special visits from God. Read about them in Genesis 28:10-22 and Genesis 32:22-32. The first encounter with God occurred when he was fleeing from Esau; the second occurred twenty years later when he was returning home.

a. Compare the two encounters by completing the following chart.[2]

	GENESIS 28:10-22	GENESIS 32:22-32
Where was Jacob?		
What happened?		
What reason(s) did Jacob have for being afraid?		
What was Jacob's response?		
What was the long-term result of the visit from God?		

b. How was Jacob's attitude at Bethel different from that at Peniel?

7. As we discovered in question 1, God made promises to Abraham, Isaac, and Jacob. All three responded positively to God's promises. From the references provided in the chart, write down how each of these men demonstrated faith in God's promises. Three examples have been completed for you.

ABRAHAM	ISAAC	JACOB
Genesis 24:3 *Made certain that his son did not marry a Canaanite.*	Genesis 28:1-2	
Genesis 12:8	Genesis 26:25	Genesis 35:2-3
Genesis 25:7-11	Genesis 49:30-31 *Buried in cave of Machpelah in Promised Land.*	Genesis 47:28-30, 49:29-32 *Commanded children to bury him in cave in Promised Land.*
Genesis 15:6	Genesis 28:3-4	Genesis 48:15-16
Genesis 14:20		Genesis 28:22

8. a. Read Hebrews 11:8-21. For what were Abraham, Isaac, and Jacob remembered?

b. What did these men do to be commended as men of faith?

c. Which of these practices are characteristic of your life?

d. In what ways might you develop these practices in your life?

YOUR QUESTIONS

NOTES
1. JoAnn J. Cairns, *God's Plan for the World* (Wheaton, Ill.: Lifeway, 1982), page 15.
2. Cairns, page 20.

Why Does a Loving God Allow Suffering?

Genesis 37-50; Job

Hardship and suffering are the consequences of original sin, Adam and Eve's disobedience to God. From earliest recorded history, people have associated suffering with sin. They are not surprised when a very wicked person suffers, but they are troubled when a righteous person receives undeserved or unfair treatment. Two righteous men who suffered were Joseph, Jacob's son, and Job.

DAY 1

God used Joseph, Jacob's eleventh and obviously favorite son, to preserve the Hebrew nation. The account of his life is contained in chapters 37 and 39-50 of Genesis. The amount of space devoted to his story is one indication of his importance in biblical history.

1. Read Genesis 30:1-24 and 37:1-11. What clues do you find that Joseph was unique?

2. Read Genesis 37:12-36 and 39:1-23 and list the things that happened to Joseph that you would consider unfair if they happened to you.

BONUS QUESTION
Imagine that you are in Joseph's situation as described in Genesis 39. Write a letter of complaint to "Heaven's Hall of Justice".

DAY 2

3. Quickly read Genesis 40-50 to learn about Joseph's life after he was imprisoned. You may want to use a modern paraphrase of the Bible.

   a. As you read the Scriptures listed in the following chart, summarize what occurred. Then record how God used the event. In some cases, the Bible states specifically how God used events for good; in others, you may draw conclusions from the context.

SCRIPTURE	EVENT	HOW GOD USED IT FOR GOOD
Genesis 37:2-11	*Joseph brags to his family about his dreams.*	*His family was able to see how God had planned to save them from famine.*
Genesis 37:12-28	*Joseph is sold into slavery.*	*He was placed in a context where he could rise to leadership.*
Genesis 39:1-23		
Genesis 40:1-23		

SCRIPTURE	EVENT	HOW GOD USED IT FOR GOOD
Genesis 41:1-36		
Genesis 41:37-52		
Genesis 45:1-15		
Genesis 50:15-21	*Joseph's brothers plead for their lives; Joseph grants forgiveness.*	*". . . to accomplish what is now being done, the saving of many lives."*

b. Look at the third column of your chart. How did God use suffering over the years to accomplish great things?

c. How do you account for this?

d. What indications of increasing maturity do you see in Joseph between Genesis 37 and 50?

e. How might Joseph's sufferings have aided the process?

4. Joseph is not the only case of an individual who matured as a result of suffering. Job, who lived long before Abraham, also did not know why he suffered. Read about his two tests in Job 1-2.

a. What kind of person was he (Job 1:1-5)?

b. List the different ways in which Job suffered.

Test 1:
Job 1:13-15

Job 1:16

Job 1:17

Job 1:18-19

Test 2:
Job 2:7-8

Job 2:9

c. How did Job respond to God during his suffering (Job 2:10)?

d. What does this tell you about him?

5. a. Three of Job's friends tried to advise him. Summarize each person's arguments as to the cause of Job's troubles and suggestions for resolving those troubles.

FRIEND	CAUSE OF TROUBLE	SUGGESTIONS
Eliphaz	Job 4:7-8, 5:8	
Bildad	Job 8:3-6	
Zophar	Job 11:1-6, 13-15	

b. How did Job respond to the analysis of his friends (Job 27:1-6)?

c. How did Job evaluate himself (Job 32:1)?

DAY 4

6. a. Another of Job's acquaintances, a young man named Elihu, rebuked Job. Why did Elihu become angry (Job 32:2-3, 34:5-6)?

b. Read Elihu's words in Job 36:22-33. How was his approach different from that of Job's other friends?

33

7. a. What was the substance of God's reply to Job's questions in Job 38:1-40:2?

b. What did Job learn from his experience? (Job 40:4-5, 42:1-6)?

DAY 5

8. Both Joseph and Job were righteous, and yet both of them suffered. Their suffering must have seemed harsh and unfair to them. How did their suffering fit into God's long-range plans (see questions 3 and 7)?

Job

Joseph

9. How would you reply to a person who asked, "How could a loving God . . ."?

YOUR QUESTIONS

How Does a Faithless Person Live?

Selected passages from Genesis 12-50

A special nation was born when Abraham obeyed God's call and left Ur. Although Abraham was to be the father of the nation, only a small percentage of his off-spring were to become a part of this nation. The descendants of Lot, Ishmael, and Esau were excluded. The faithlessness of these three men stands in sharp contrast to the faith of Abraham, Isaac, and Jacob. As you complete this week's assignment, you may want to refer to "A Chronology of Genesis 12-50" (page 42).

DAY 1

1. What can we discover about Lot from the following Scripture references?

    Genesis 11:27

    Genesis 11:31, 12:4-5

2. Read about Lot's life in Genesis 13:1-14:16 and 18:1-19:38.

    a. List the places where Lot loved.

    Genesis 13:5

    Genesis 13:12

Genesis 14:12

Genesis 19:1

b. For what reason(s) do you think Lot made those moves?

c. How is Lot's character reflected in his behavior as reported in the following passages of Scripture?

Genesis 13:10-13

Genesis 19:1-3

Genesis 19:6-8

Genesis 19:12-14

Genesis 19:15-16

Genesis 19:17-22

DAY 2

3. Read the account of Ishmael and Hagar in Genesis 16:1-16, 17:15-27, 21:8-21, and 25:7-18. Describe the relationships between

Sarai and Hagar.

Ishmael and Sarah.

Isaac and Ishmael.

Ishmael and Abraham.

Hagar and Ishmael.

4. Hagar, Sarah's personal maid, mothered a child for Abraham and Sarah. Twice she left, fearful and discouraged—the object of Sarah's envy. Both times God spoke to her and gave her special help. Compare these two incidents, keeping in mind that they were more than fourteen years apart.

	GENESIS 16:1-16	GENESIS 21:8-21
Why did Hagar leave Sarai?		
Where was she when God spoke to her?		
How did God help her?		

	GENESIS 16:1-16	GENESIS 21:8-21
What did she do after God appeared to her?		
What did God tell Hagar about Ishmael?		

DAY 3

5. Read about Esau in Genesis 25:19-34, 26:34-27:45, and 28:6-9.

    a. How were Jacob and Esau similar in character?

    b. Name at least four ways in which Jacob and Esau were different.

JACOB	ESAU

    c. What did God predict for Esau (Genesis 25:23)?

    d. How does Isaac's blessing in Genesis 27:39-40 affirm God's prediction?

6. a. How did Esau respond to Jacob and the values of Isaac, Rebekah, and Jacob in each of the following events?

Genesis 25:29-34

Genesis 27:30-41

Genesis 33:1-16

Genesis 35:28-29

b. How might you explain the change in Esau's attitude toward Jacob between chapter 27 and chapter 33?

c. What part do you believe Esau played in the development of Jacob's character? (You may want to review lesson 3.)

DAY 4

7. Although Laban was not a descendant of Abraham, he was a relative who played an important part in two generations. Read Genesis 11:29 and chapters 24, 29, 30, and 31.

a. How was Laban related to

Abraham?

Isaac?

Jacob?

b. How would you describe his character? Support your description with Scripture.

c. Why was it to Leah's and Rachael's advantage to move away from him (Genesis 31:14-16)?

DAY 5

8. Select Lot, Ishmael, Esau, or Laban for study. Review the account of his life and answer the following questions:

a. How was he related to Abraham, Isaac, or Jacob?

b. What kind of person (nationality, religion, or whatever is mentioned) did he marry?

c. How did the individual demonstrate belief or lack of belief in God?

d. How was his behavior different from the behavior you want to exhibit in your own life?

e. How was it similar?

f. Write a short biography (one or two paragraphs) of the character you have chosen, including the information from the previous questions.

9. Review your answers to questions 1-8.

   a. What attitudes, deeds, or values do you see exemplified in Lot, Ishmael, Esau, and Laban?

   b. Circle the characteristics that you would associate with a faithless person.

   c. Underline any of these traits that you see in your own life.

   d. State one specific thing you can do to apply the principles of faith (lesson 2) to a faithless tendency in your life.

YOUR QUESTIONS

A CHRONOLOGY OF GENESIS 12-50				
Abraham's age	Isaac's age	Jacob's age	Joseph's age	
75				Abraham moves from Haran to Canaan
				Abraham goes to Egypt
				Abraham and Lot separate
				Abraham rescues Lot
				God's covenant with Abraham
85				Sarah gives Abraham her maidservant, Hagar
86				Birth of Ishmael
99				Circumcision instituted; Abraham's and Sarah's names changed
				Hospitality extended to strangers
				Destruction of Sodom
				Abraham lies to Abimilech
100	0			Birth of Isaac
				Isaac offered as a sacrifice
128	28			Death of Sarah
140	40			Isaac's marriage to Rebekah
160	60	0		Birth of Jacob and Esau
175	75	15		Death of Abraham
				Esau's sale of his birthright
		40		Esau's marriage to Hittite women
				Jacob receives Esau's blessing
				Jacob's flight
				Jacob spends twenty years with Laban; birth of twelve sons and one daughter
				Death of Rachel; return of Jacob to Canaan
	180	120		Death of Isaac
		120	17	Joseph sold into slavery
		130	27	Jacob's arrival in Egypt
		147	44	Death of Jacob
			110	Death of Joseph (approximately 93 years after his arrival in Egypt and 66 years after Jacob's death)

LESSON SIX

How Does God Work to Deliver His People?

Exodus 1-14

DAY 1

Nearly four hundred years elapsed between the time of Joseph, described in Genesis 41-50, and the time of Moses, described in Exodus 1. Meanwhile Joseph died, but Jacob's descendants remained in Goshen, a fertile area in the northern part of Egypt.

1. Compare the descendants of Jacob at the time of Joseph with their descendants at the time of Moses.

	TIME OF JOSEPH Genesis 46:26-47:12	TIME OF MOSES Exodus 1:1-2:23, 12:37
Number of Hebrews		
Occupation		
Treatment received from the Egyptians		
Relationship with Pharaoh		
Probable attitude of Hebrews toward life		
Financial status of the Hebrews		

Study your completed chart. Summarize the changes that occurred over the 400-year period.

_____

2. Moses was God's man to free the Hebrews (or Israelites) from the Egyptians. Read about his early life in Exodus 2:1-25.

a. What clues can you find to Moses' lifestyle

in Egypt?

in Midian?

b. From where did Moses' early religious influences come (Exodus 2:1-10)?

c. What religious influences were present in Midian (Exodus 2:11-15)?

d. How do you think Moses' training and experiences prepared him to lead the Hebrews out of Egypt?

e. How did Moses relate to the rest of the Hebrew people?

_____

3. a. Read Exodus 3:1-4:17. What signs did God give to Moses?

3:1-4

4:1-4

4:6-7

b. Why do you think Moses needed the miraculous signs God gave him?

c. Why was God's identification of Himself in Exodus 3:6 significant? (For further insight, consult a study Bible or commentary.)

d. Why do you think Moses hid his face from God?

DAY 2

4. a. What instructions did God give Moses?

Exodus 3:14-15

Exodus 3:16-17

Exodus 3:18-20

b. What misgivings did Moses express?

Exodus 3:11

Exodus 4:1

Exodus 4:10

Exodus 4:13

c. What other reasons might Moses have had for not wanting to return to Egypt?

d. How do you think you would have responded in the same situation?

---

5. Read Exodus 4:18-6:9. How did the following people respond to Moses?

Jethro (Exodus 4:18)

Aaron (Exodus 4:27-29)

The elders of the Israelites (Exodus 4:29-31)

Pharaoh (Exodus 5:1-9)

The Israelites (Exodus 5:10-21)

6. a. Read Exodus 7:14-12:30 and complete the following chart.

PLAGUE	DESCRIPTION OF PLAGUE	RESULT OF PLAGUE	PHARAOH'S REACTION
1 Exodus 7:14-24	*Water changed to blood.*	*Fish died. No drinking water for the Egyptians.*	*His heart became hard.*
2 Exodus 7:25-8:15	*Frogs covered the land.*	*Frogs ate food and became general nuisance. May have carried disease.*	*He hardened his heart.*
3 Exodus 8:16-19			
4 Exodus 8:20-32			
5 Exodus 9:1-7			
6 Exodus 9:8-12			
7 Exodus 9:13-35			
8 Exodus 10:1-20			

PLAGUE	DESCRIPTION OF PLAGUE	RESULT OF PLAGUE	PHARAOH'S REACTION
9 Exodus 10:21-29			
10 Exodus 11:1-12:42			

b. How did the Egyptian magicians respond to the plagues?

Exodus 7:22

Exodus 8:7

Exodus 8:18-19

Exodus 9:11

DAY 4

7. a. Read Exodus 14. What supernatural phenomena are recorded in this chapter?

b. How do you think the ten plagues and drowning of the Egyptian army affected the Egyptian economy?

8. a. Genesis 15:13-14 contains a prophecy God made to Abraham before Isaac was born. What did God say would happen?

b. How was this prophecy fulfilled?

DAY 5

9. Read the song that Moses and the Israelites sang in Exodus 15:1-21.

    a. How is God described (look for adjectives)?

    b. What did God do (look for active verbs)?

10. a. How is Moses described in Deuteronomy 34:10-12?

    b. How did Moses' character change from the time God appeared to him in the burning bush until his death? List at least four points of contrast.

11. a. Review this lesson and list how God expressed His faithfulness to the

    Israelites.

    Moses.

b. List at least six specific ways God has expressed His faithfulness to you.

YOUR QUESTIONS

How Does God Discipline His People?

Exodus 14-17, 32; Numbers 11, 13-14, 20-25;
Deuteronomy 1-3, 34

DAY 1

1. After their miraculous delivery from Egypt, the Israelites enthusiastically headed for Canaan, the land promised to Abraham. Their enthusiasm, however, was short-lived. They spent forty years wandering in the Sinai peninsula before they reached the Promised Land.

     The history of the wilderness wanderings is recorded in detail in Exodus and Numbers. A number of events might be called "change points" because life for the Israelites was different after each of those events occurred. Read each Scripture passage and briefly state what happened and how you think that event might have changed the lives of the Hebrews.

BRIEF DESCRIPTION OF EVENT	HOW EVENT AFFECTED ISRAELITES
Exodus 14:1-31 *The Israelites crossed Red Sea through God's miraculous intervention; Egyptians were drowned in sea.*	*Egypt was no longer a threat; the Israelites were an independent nation.*
Exodus 19:1-20:26	

BRIEF DESCRIPTION OF EVENT	HOW EVENT AFFECTED ISRAELITES
Numbers 13:1-14:45	
Deuteronomy 34:1-12	

DAYS 2 and 3

2. No one can cross a desert without encountering difficulties. We can discover how the Hebrews reacted to the difficulties by completing the chart on the following page. Study the Scripture portions, describe each problem encountered by the Hebrews, record their response to the problem, and note God's response to them.

SCRIPTURE	DESCRIPTION OF PROBLEM	BEHAVIOR OF HEBREWS	GOD'S RESPONSE
1 Exodus 14:10-31	*They were trapped, with the Egyptians pursuing them from behind and the sea in front of them.*	*Accused Moses of taking them into the desert to be killed. Feared the Lord when they saw His power.*	*Miraculously parted the sea so that they crossed on dry land.*
2 Exodus 15:22-26			
3 Exodus 16:1-35			

SCRIPTURE	DESCRIPTION OF PROBLEM	BEHAVIOR OF HEBREWS	GOD'S RESPONSE
4 Exodus 17:1-7			
5 Exodus 32:1-35	*Moses was up on the mountain, out of sight; the people wanted a visible leader or god.*	*Made a golden calf and worshipped it, claiming it had delivered them from Egypt.*	*3,000 people slain by Levis at Moses' command.*
6 Numbers 11:1-3			
7 Numbers 11:4-34			
8 Numbers 13:1-3, 17-33, 14:1-38			

3. a. Look at God's responses to the Israelites' behavior. In which cases do you feel that God demonstrated mercy? (Use the numbers from the chart—1, 2, 3, etc.)

b. In which cases do you feel that God was severe?

c. What pattern do you see in God's responses to the rebellious Israelites?

d. How do you think the events in Exodus 19-20 demonstrate the mercy or wrath of God?

---

4. a. List the ten commandments from Exodus 20:3-17.

1)

2)

3)

4)

5)

6)

7)

8)

9)

10)

b. Underline the commandments that the Israelites violated.

DAY 4

5. a. Study Numbers 20:1-13. Why, in your opinion, did Moses strike the rock when God had told him to speak to it?

b. How did God respond to him?

c. How can we explain God's response (see James 3:1)?

d. Read the description of Moses death in Deuteronomy 34. In what ways was Moses an exceptional man?

6. a. Read the account of Balaam in Numbers 22:1-25:18. What do you discover about God?

the Israelites?

Moab (see also Genesis 19:30-38)?

sorcery?

b. How did the Moabites finally succeed in weakening the Israelite strength?

DAY 5

7. Review this lesson and lesson 6.

   a. What miracles did God perform for the Hebrews?

   b. Based on the chart on pages 52-53, what was the main way in which the Hebrews demonstrated their rebelliousness?

   c. In what ways did God punish the Hebrews?

8. The Israelites' complaints and grumbling were only symptoms of more basic conditions. What was the real problem, identified in Hebrews 3:7-4:11?

9. As the Israelites became accustomed to God's discipline, they began to develop self-discipline.

a. Why does God discipline?

b. What can we learn about how to respond to His discipline from Hebrews 12:4-16?

YOUR QUESTIONS

How Can a Person Relate to God?

Exodus 19, 25-28, 33, 40; Leviticus 1, 10-19, 23, 26;
Numbers 28; Deuteronomy 16

DAY 1

Life was simple for Abraham, Isaac, and Jacob. They lived in tents, caring for their flocks, and moving whenever they needed fresh pasture. They functioned as multi-generational family units. Their worship of God was also simple and tailored to their needs. From time-to-time, they built altars to God and offered sacrifices, but beyond this there was no established religious practice.

One reason for the simplicity and individuality of religious worship for the patriarchs was the small number of people. Only sixty-six Hebrews went to Egypt in Joseph's time. Four hundred years later, 600,000 Israelites left for Canaan. That nation needed an organized religious form. During the two years that the Israelites camped at the base of Mt. Sinai, God instructed them. A tabernacle or sanctuary was constructed as God's dwelling place, priests were appointed, and a systematic pattern for worship and sacrifice was established.

---

1. a. Read Exodus 19. What did God promise the Israelites (verse 3-6)?

b. What conditions did God attach to these promises (verse 5)?

c. How were the people required to prepare before God spoke to them (verses 14-15)?

d. What physical phenomena were present when God spoke (verses 16-19)?

DAY 2

2. Under God's direction, the Israelites constructed a tabernacle. The instructions were explicit, not only for the tabernacle itself, but also for the furnishings and the surrounding courtyard.

a. The following chart includes the major items associated with the tabernacle. Complete the chart, using the Scripture references given in the left column.

SCRIPTURE	ITEM	SPECIFIC PARTS MENTIONED IN CONNECTION WITH ITEM	MATERIALS USED IN CONSTRUCTION	PURPOSE OF ITEM
Exodus 25:10-22	Ark (chest)	Rings, poles, testimony tablets, cover, cherubims		
Exodus 25:23-30	Table	Rings, poles, plates, bread of the Presence, pitchers, bowls, ladles		
Exodus 25:31-40, 27:20-21				
Exodus 26:1-37				

SCRIPTURE	ITEM	SPECIFIC PARTS MENTIONED IN CON-NECTION WITH ITEM	MATERIALS USED IN CONSTRUCTION	PURPOSE OF ITEM
Exodus 27:1-8				
Exodus 27:9-19				

b. How did God show His approval when the tabernacle was completed (Exodus 40:34-38)?

c. Look at your completed chart. What are your impressions of the tabernacle?

DAY 3

3. a. Priests were appointed as religious leaders of the nation. How could a man become a priest (Exodus 28:1, 43; Numbers 3:10)?

b. How did the priests dress (Exodus 28:2-5)?

c. What did their duties include (Leviticus 1:7-8, 10:10-11)?

d. What additional insights does Hebrews 5:1-4 provide us about priests?

4. a. Read Leviticus 10:1-11. What did Nadab and Abihu do?

   b. How did God respond?

   c. What did God forbid the priests to do when He punished Nadab and Abihu (verses 6-7)?

   d. How do you think these restrictions might have been difficult for Aaron?

BONUS QUESTION
Write an entry in Aaron's diary for the day Nadab and Abihu died. Describe the events from Aaron's perspective; include his feelings as you imagine them.

5. Sacrifices were offered on the altar daily. There were several types of offerings, but all of the offerings for sin required an animal sacrifice. Read the instructions for burnt offerings in Leviticus 1:1-17.

   a. What qualifications for the animal were required (verses 3, 10, 14)?

   b. Outline the steps involved in sacrificing a ram (verses 4-9):

6. God set up laws on many different subjects. What was the subject of the laws in each of the following passages?

Leviticus 11

Leviticus 12

Leviticus 13

Leviticus 16

Leviticus 18, 20:13-16

Leviticus 19:26b, 20:6, 27

7. The Israelites were told to observe three major feasts each year. All men who were ceremonially clean and physically able were expected to attend. The importance of these feasts was reiterated again and again.

a. From the Scripture describing each, note the purpose or significance of that feast.

SCRIPTURE	NAMES GIVEN TO FEAST	PURPOSE OR SIGNIFICANCE OF FEAST
Exodus 23:15 Leviticus 23:5-8 Numbers 28:16-25 Deuteronomy 16:1-8	Passover Unleavened Bread	
Exodus 23:16a Leviticus 23:9-22 Numbers 28:26-31 Deuteronomy 16:9-12	Weeks First Fruits Pentecost Harvest	

SCRIPTURE	NAMES GIVEN TO FEAST	PURPOSE OR SIGNIFICANCE OF FEAST
Exodus 23:16b Leviticus 23:33-43 Numbers 29:12-38 Deuteronomy 16:13-15	Tabernacles Booths Ingathering	

b. How do you think the observance of these feasts may have helped the Hebrews to become established as a nation?

8. a. What did God promise to those who obey His laws (Leviticus 26:3-13)?

b. What did God say He would do to those who disobey His laws (Leviticus 26:14-46)?

DAY 5

9. How is the Old Testament law fulfilled in the New Testament (the basis for your faith)?

	OLD TESTAMENT	NEW TESTAMENT
How you approach God (Exodus 33:7-11; Leviticus 16:1-34; John 14:6; Hebrews 4:15-16)		

64

	OLD TESTAMENT	NEW TESTAMENT
Sacrifices for sins (Leviticus 1:3-4; Hebrews 9:27)		
Frequency of sacrifices (Hebrews 9:27)		
Characteristics of high priest (Hebrews 5:1-3, 4:14-16)		

10. a. List at least four things for which God has forgiven you.

    b. If you were living in Old Testament times, what would you need to do to obtain God's forgiveness (review question 5)?

    c. What do you need to do today to receive God's forgiveness (Hebrews 4:14-16)?

YOUR QUESTIONS

What Can God Do with Obedient People?

Joshua

DAY 1

1. When Moses died, Joshua assumed leadership of the nation. The wilderness wanderings were over, and the people were ready to enter the Promised Land.

   a. What can we discover about Joshua's early years from the following passages?

   Exodus 17:8-16

   Exodus 24:9-14

   Exodus 33:7-11

   Numbers 14:1-9, 30, 36-38

   b. List at least four adjectives that describe Joshua.

2. a. Read Joshua 1:1-9 and list the specific instructions God gave to Joshua.

b. What did God promise Joshua?

DAY 2

3. Read Joshua 2-6. Although Joshua had been commissioned to lead the Israelites in the conquest of Canaan, there were formidable barriers to overcome. From Joshua 2-6, name two major barriers, and why they were problems. (You will complete the last column in the chart later.)

SCRIPTURE	BARRIER	REASON BARRIER WAS A PROBLEM	HOW THE PROBLEM WAS RESOLVED
3:1-4:18			
5:13-6:27			

4. From Joshua 3:1-17, what were the stages in crossing the Jordan River?

Verse 5

Verses 6, 15

Verse 16

Verse 17a

Verse 17b

DAY 3

5. a. What steps did Joshua follow in capturing Jericho?

Joshua 2:1-24

Joshua 5:1-8

Joshua 5:10-12

Joshua 5:13-6:5

Joshua 6:6-21

Joshua 6:22-25

b. Complete the chart in question 3.

6. Hebrews 11:31 cites Rahab as an example of faith.

a. What evidence of her faith do you find in Joshua 2:2-24?

b. What did she believe about God?

c. How was she rewarded (Joshua 6:22-23)?

DAY 4

---

7. a. Read Joshua 5:13-6:27, 10:16-43, and 11:1-12. In what order did he attack the northern, central, and southern sections of the country? What cities did he attack in each section? You will probably want to consult a map.

First section

Major cities

Second section

Major cities

Third section

Major cities

b. Why do you think Joshua used this military strategy?

8. Even though the Israelites, as a nation, were obedient to God when they entered the Promised Land, they made mistakes during the conquest of Canaan. Study the following Scripture passages and complete the chart.

	JOSHUA 7:1-26	JOSHUA 9:1-27	JUDGES 1:27-2:3
Mistake			
Person(s) responsible			
Penalty			

9. a. Read Joshua's farewell address in Joshua 24. On the basis of this address, what adjectives can you add to the list you developed in question 1?

b. What resulted from the leadership of Moses and Joshua (Joshua 24:13)?

10. a. What was characteristic of the people who settled in the Promised Land (Joshua 24:31)?

b. How were they different from those who died in the wilderness?

c. How did the people know what God expected of them?

d. How do we know what God expects of us today?

BONUS QUESTION
Write a news bulletin (one or two paragraphs) to cover any one of the following incidents:

a. Crossing the Jordan (Joshua 3:1-4:21)
b. The destruction of Jericho (Joshua 5:13-6:27)
c. The two battles with Ai (Joshua 7:1-8:29) (From the perspective of an outsider with no knowledge of Achan's sin)
d. The sin and punishment of Achan (written by an Israelite) (Joshua 7:1-26)
e. The defeat of the Amorites (Joshua 10:1-28)

YOUR QUESTIONS

Why Does a Righteous Nation Become Evil?

Judges; Ruth; 1 Samuel 1-7

When Moses died, Joshua was appointed by God to lead the people. He led an obedient nation of more than six hundred thousand soldiers, plus Levites, plus women and children, in the conquest of the Promised Land. All of the major cities were destroyed, and Israel was established in her own land with her own special identity.

When Joshua died, however, no successor was appointed. As long as the group who had originally invaded Canaan was alive, the people followed the customs and rules of conduct they had followed under Joshua. But when that group died, "everyone did as he saw fit" (Judges 17:6).

We might expect the nation to continue generation after generation, living as they had been taught under Moses and Joshua. But the period of the judges demonstrates a completely different trend.

DAY 1

1. Joshua's death ushered in a period of approximately four hundred years, commonly known as the time of the judges. Judges 2:1-3:6 describes what happened during this time. Read the passage and answer the following questions:

   a. What sins did the Israelites commit?

   b. How did God respond to their sin?

2. What steps occurred in the relationship of Israel to God and to the surrounding nations?

Judges 2:11-13

Judges 2:14-15

Judges 2:16-18

Judges 2:19

The life of the nation in that era might be expressed by the following cycle:

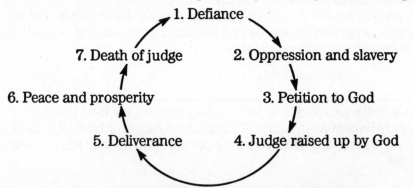

1. Defiance
2. Oppression and slavery
3. Petition to God
4. Judge raised up by God
5. Deliverance
6. Peace and prosperity
7. Death of judge

1. The Israelites defied God by deliberately disobeying His laws.
2. They were attacked by surrounding nations. Their fields were raided, they were killed, and members of their families were captured.
3. They cried out to God in their distress.
4. God raised up a judge to lead them to deliverance.
5. They were delivered from their enemies.
6. They enjoyed a period of peace and prosperity.
7. The judge died.

This cycle was repeated at least seven times during the four hundred years.

3. Read the scriptural account of each of the judges in the following chart. Then complete the chart.

SCRIPTURE	SINS(S) OF THE PEOPLE	CONQUERING NATION AND LENGTH OF ENSLAVEMENT (IF GIVEN)	NAME OF JUDGE	LENGTH OF PEACE FOR ISRAEL
Judges 3:7-11	*Idolatry*	*Aram—8 years*	*Othniel*	*40 years*
Judges 3:12-30				
Judges 4:1-5:31				
Judges 6:1-8:35				
Judges 10:6-11:40				
Judges 13:1-16:31				

DAY 3

4. Two of the better known judges were Gideon (Judges 6:1-8:35) and Samson (Judges 13:1-16:31). Select one of these men and read the account of his life. Then answer the following questions:

a. What indications do you find that Israel needed a judge?

b. What can you discover about his parents?

c. How would you describe his spiritual commitment throughout his life?

d. What miracles did God perform through him?

e. How did God use him to deliver Israel?

f. Why do you think he was cited as an example of faith in Hebrews 11:32-34?

---

5. Samuel was the last of the judges. Read about him in 1 Samuel 1-7. How was he unusual?

1 Samuel 1:1-20

1 Samuel 1:21-28

1 Samuel 3:1-19

---

6. Briefly summarize the cycle of the judges in 1 Samuel 1-7 by stating in one or two sentences what happened in each of the following Scripture passages:

Defiance (1 Samuel 2:12-36)

Oppression and slavery (1 Samuel 4:1-22)

Petition to God (1 Samuel 7:2)

Judge raised up (1 Samuel 7:3-4)

Deliverance (1 Samuel 7:5-12)

Peace and Prosperity (1 Samuel 7:13-17

DAY 4

Ruth lived one or two generations before Samuel during the time of the judges. Skim Judges 19-21, then quickly read the book of Ruth.

---

7. a. What was Ruth's nationality?

b. What barriers to a relationship with God do you think her nationality created?

---

8. Trace the steps God used to change Ruth's life.

Ruth 1:3-4

Ruth 1:5

Ruth 1:6-7

Ruth 1:8-18

Ruth 2:2

Ruth 2:8-23

Ruth 4:9-13a

Ruth 4:13b

---

9. a. What do you think was the relationship between the sins listed in question 3 and the failure of Israel to drive out the foreign people?

b. How do Jeremiah 17:9 and Romans 3:9-19 help to explain why the Israelites continued to return to their sins?

---

10. a. What sins do you see Christians committing today because they have close relationships with people of other religious persuasions?

b. In what ways are you or have you been influenced by those who do not share your spiritual perspective?

c. Read Romans 12:1-3. What can you do to prevent conformity to the pattern of this world?

11. a. Review this lesson. Then explain why a good nation can become evil.

b. Read Colossians 3:1-17. What can you do to imitate Christ in an ungodly society?

YOUR QUESTIONS

Why Is Total Obedience Necessary?

Life of Saul: 1 Samuel 8:1-19:24, 28:1-25, 31:1-13

DAY 1

Under God's leadership, the nation of Israel changed from a mass of indecisive slaves to an established, recognized kingdom. Surrounding peoples lived in fear and respect of her; they knew that a supreme God looked after Israel.

God's intention was that His people should be different from other nations. They were to worship Him alone and depend on Him alone for their safety and food. The priests were responsible for the leadership of the nation, but God was their ruler. Even the judges raised up by God were His representatives, not the rulers, of the nation.

When Samuel was old, the nation decided they needed a king. God gave them what they wanted. Saul was the first of three men appointed by God to rule the nation; each of the three kings had a reign of approximately forty years.

---

1. a. Read 1 Samuel 8:1-22. What reasons did the people give for wanting a king?

b. What did God say was the real reason the people wanted a king?

---

2. a. What do you discover about Samuel's sons (1 Samuel 8:1-5)?

b. Why were their appointments as judges unusual? (You may want to refer to lesson 10 in responding to this question.)

c. How did Samuel respond to the request for a king (verses 4-7)?

d. Imagine yourself in Samuel's position when the elders of Israel asked for a king (verses 4-5). How would you have felt?

3. From your reading of 1 Samuel 8 name some of the advantages and disadvantages of having a king appointed.

   Advantages

   Disadvantages

DAY 2

4. Read about Saul's appointment as king in 1 Samuel 9-10. From your reading, how would you describe him.

5. a. What signs did Samuel give to Saul about his appointment (1 Samuel 10:1-7)?

b. Why do you think Samuel gave Saul so many signs?

c. How did God affirm Saul's appointment as king?

1 Samuel 10:9

1 Samuel 10:24-26

DAY 3

6. a. What events marked the beginning of Saul's reign (1 Samuel 11:1-15)?

b. Where did Saul receive his motivation?

c. How did Saul's behavior affect the nation?

7. Saul certainly started out well. He tried to please God and he united the twelve tribes into one army. But during his reign, his allegiance changed.

a. How did he displease God in each of the following incidents?

1 Samuel 13:1-14

1 Samuel 15:1-35

b. What resulted from Saul's sin?

1 Samuel 13:14

1 Samuel 15:26-28

1 Samuel 16:14

c. Why do you think the punishment was so severe?

David was born ten years after Saul became king. When David was a young man (possibly a teenager), Samuel anointed him as Saul's successor. For most of his remaining years, Saul employed all of his energies in unsuccessful attempts to kill David.

DAY 4

8. a. Trace Saul's experiences with the Spirit of God and evil spirits by completing the following chart.

SPIRIT CONTROLLING SAUL	SAUL'S SUBSEQUENT BEHAVIOR
1 Samuel 10:9-10	
1 Samuel 11:6-8	
1 Samuel 16:14-15	
1 Samuel 18:10-11	

b. Study your chart. How did the Spirit of God and evil spirits influence the man?

---

9. a. Read 1 Samuel 28. What can you learn about Saul from this incident?

b. What did Saul learn from the witch?

---

10. Read 1 Samuel 31. Write Saul's obituary for a local news-paper. Include his background, his accomplishments, and a brief description of how he died.

DAY 5

---

11. a. Read 1 Samuel 15. How did Saul try to justify his actions?

b. How did Samuel respond?

c. Why did Saul want to be forgiven?

Verse 25

Verse 30

d. What did God require of Saul?

---

12. Saul tried to bend God's laws to suit himself. Study the following references and complete the chart.

WHAT SAUL WANTED	WHAT GOD REQUIRED
1 Samuel 13:1-14	
1 Samuel 15:1-9	
1 Samuel 15:22	

---

13. Using a concordance, find four verses from the Bible on obedience. List each reference below and briefly summarize its teaching.

REFERENCE	TEACHING ON OBEDIENCE
1.	
2.	
3.	
4.	

14. a. List several ways you think people try to substitute other actions for obedience to God.

b. Underline any of the above that pose a temptation to you.

c. Look at question 13. What advice can you give yourself from the Bible?

d. How do you think God would have you begin to carry out your advice this week?

YOUR QUESTIONS

How Is a Man or a Woman of God Trained?

Life of David, Part 1: 1 Samuel 16:1-27:12;
2 Samuel 1:1-27

DAY 1

1. Read 1 Samuel 16. What do we learn about David from this chapter?

   a. His family

   b. His appearance

   c. His heart (spiritual commitment)

   d. His abilities and experience

2. a. Summarize the story in 1 Samuel 17.

b. How do you think David was viewed by each of the following people?

His father

His brothers

Saul

Goliath

c. How did David demonstrate his faith in God?

DAY 2

3. Write a short newspaper article about the defeat of Goliath. Write from the perspective of one of the characters involved (even a nameless one). Use your creative genius to come up with an original title or use one of the following:

"Saul Runs Scared" (from the perspective of Saul's assistant)
"Showoff Gets Lucky" (from the perspective of David's brother)
"Strange Weapon Topples Giant" (from the perspective of a Philistine soldier)
"Youth Wins for God" (from the perspective of Samuel)

4. a. From 1 Samuel 18:1-30, what responsibility did Saul give to David?

b. How did the people react to David?

c. How did Saul react to David (verse 12)?

d. Why do you think Saul reacted that way (verses 12-16, 28-29)?

DAY 3

5. David spent many years as a fugitive, fleeing from Saul. To summarize those years, use the chart. (Some spaces will remain blank.)

SCRIPTURE	SAUL'S TREATMENT OF DAVID	DAVID'S TREATMENT OF SAUL	HOW DAVID WAS DELIVERED
1 Samuel 18:10-11, 19:8-10	*On three occasions, Saul tried to kill David by hurling a spear at him while he was playing the harp.*		*He eluded Saul each time.*
1 Samuel 19:11-17	*Saul sent men to capture David at his home so that Saul might kill him.*		*David's wife lowered him down to safety from a window and he escaped.*
1 Samuel 19:18-24			

SCRIPTURE	SAUL'S TREATMENT OF DAVID	DAVID'S TREATMENT OF SAUL	HOW DAVID WAS DELIVERED
1 Samuel 3:7-13			
1 Samuel 23:14-28			
1 Samuel 24:1-22			
1 Samuel 26:1-25			

6. a. Read 2 Samuel 1:1-27. How did David react to Saul's death?

Verses 11-12

Verses 13-16

Verses 17-27

b. What can you learn about David from his response to Saul's death?

c. How did David's reaction to Saul's death compare with what you might have expected his reaction to be?

DAY 4

7. Jonathan was in line to be Saul's successor; but God chose David for the position, and Jonathan was fully aware of God's choice. The relationship between David and Jonathan is a model of love and friendship.

a. If you had been Jonathan, how do you think you would have reacted when you learned that David was to inherit your throne?

b. What was the relationship between Jonathan and David in each of the following situations?

1 Samuel 18:1-4

1 Samuel 19:1-7

1 Samuel 20:1-42

1 Samuel 23:16-18

BONUS QUESTION
Use your concordance to learn all you can about Jonathan. Make a list of all that he did. Based on that list, summarize his character, his accomplishments, and his abilities.

DAY 5

8. From your previous study, how did Saul and Jonathan differ in their relationships with David (List at least two points of contrast)?

SAUL	JONATHAN

9. a. How do you think the difficulties of David's early life affected his military and spiritual leadership?

b. What hardships, misunderstandings, or persecution are you facing today, or have you experienced in the past?

c. Read James 1:2-12. How can the hardships you listed help to mold you into the image of Christ?

d. Knowing the benefits that hardships can produce in your life, how should you respond

to hardship?

to God?

YOUR QUESTIONS

How Does a Man or a Woman of God Behave?

Life of David, Part 2: 2 Samuel 11:1-14:25,
1 Kings 1, 1 Chronicles 21

DAY 1

David was a young man when Samuel anointed him as Saul's successor, yet many years passed before David actually became king of the twelve tribes. For much of this time, David lived in the wilderness, hiding from Saul. His life was frequently threatened. A group of outcasts and criminals joined him. He hardly had the life of an up-and-coming king! Finally, Saul was dead, and things should have begun to improve. But even with Saul dead, David had opposition; two more years would pass before the nation acknowledged him as king.

---

1. a. The major events in David's life from his anointing by Samuel to his acceptance by the nation are recorded in the following scripture passages. Trace those events by stating in one or two sentences what occurred in each instance.

1 Samuel 16:13

1 Samuel 19:1

1 Samuel 31:6

2 Samuel 2:4

2 Samuel 2:10

All the tribes of Israel except Judah acknowledged Saul's son Ish-bosheth as their king.

2 Samuel 2:12-17

David's army defeated the army of Israel.

2 Samuel 4:5-6

2 Samuel 5:1-4

b. Why do you think God permitted so much opposition to David when He had promised David the throne?

---

2. At the end of Saul's reign, Israel was overrun by the Philistines. David's first task was to strengthen the nation's military position.

   a. What cities and nations did he conquer?

2 Samuel 5:6-10

2 Samuel 5:17-25

2 Samuel 8:2

2 Samuel 8:5-6

2 Samuel 8:12

b. Locate each of these cities and nations on a map in your Bible or a Bible atlas. What can you say about their locations in relationship to Israel?

---

3. As soon as Jerusalem was established as the political center of Israel, David made arrangements to move the Ark of the Covenant to Jerusalem.

a. Why was the Ark important (Exodus 25:22)?

b. The Ark, which had been captured by the Philistines during the days of Eli and Samuel, was held by a number of groups before David finally moved it to Jerusalem. Complete the following chart.

WHO POSSESSED THE ARK	PLACE	EFFECT ON PEOPLE WHO HELD IT
1 Samuel 4:1-11, 5:1-7 Philistines	Ashod	Ashdod devastation, tumors. Statue of Dagon fell face-down before the Ark.
1 Samuel 5:8-9		

WHO POSSESSED THE ARK	PLACE	EFFECT ON PEOPLE WHO HELD IT
1 Samuel 5:10-12		
1 Samuel 6:1-20		
1 Samuel 6:21, 7:1-2		

4. What instructions had God given for transporting the Ark from one place to another (Exodus 25:10-16, Numbers 4:4-20)?

5. Second Samuel 6:1-23 describes moving the Ark to Jerusalem. Read this passage and answer the following questions:

a. How were God's instructions for moving the Ark violated (2 Samuel 6:6-9)?

b. What resulted from this violation?

c. How did David react to God's punishment (2 Samuel 6:8-10)?

d. What is your reaction to David's behavior?

e. What did he do to correct the situation (1 Chronicles 15:2, 12-15)?

6. a. How did David celebrate the return of the Ark (2 Samuel 6:5,14-16)?

b. What was Michal's response to David's behavior (2 Samuel 6:16,20)?

c. What is your reaction

   to David's behavior?

   to Michal's behavior?

DAY 3

7. Read 2 Samuel 9. What can you learn about David's character from this story?

8. David committed three serious, well-known sins recorded in 2 Samuel 11-12 and 1 Chronicles 21.

   a. Complete the following chart.

SIN	GOD'S PUNISHMENT	DAVID'S REACTION
2 Samuel 11-12 1. 2.		
1 Chronicles 21 3.		

   b. How was each punishment God selected for David appropriate for each of his sins?

   c. Who suffered for David's sins?

9. Read the special instructions for kings in Deuteronomy 17:14-20. How do these instructions relate to David's sins?

10. a. Briefly summarize in 1 or 2 sentences what happened to David's family in each of the following passages:

2 Samuel 12:15-20

2 Samuel 13

2 Samuel 14:1-19:8

1 Kings 1:1-53

b. How might these events be related to David's sins (2 Samuel 12:10-14)?

11. How is David described in

1 Kings 11:4?

1 Kings 15:5?

Acts 13:22?

DAY 5

---

12. a. Read 1 Kings 2:1-12. What advice did David give to Solomon?

b. How does this charge demonstrate his character and relationship with God?

---

13. Review lessons 12 and 13 and answer the following questions:

a. What skills did David display?

b. In what ways was life difficult for David?

c. What sins did David commit?

d. How would you describe David's character and personality (list at least five adjectives)?

_____

14. a. How did David demonstrate that he was a "man after God's own heart"?

b. How might you more clearly demonstrate that you are a person after God's own heart?

c. What will you do to reflect God's character more effectively?

YOUR QUESTIONS

How Can I Worship More Effectively?

Life of David—Part 3: selected psalms

David knew God intimately. As a youth, he had spent much of his time out in the fields, alone with the family sheep and with God. He had seen and experienced the wonders of God's creation. He had learned dependence upon his God when he faced danger in the fields, when he confronted and killed Goliath, and when he lived as an exile, evading Saul.

God told Samuel that He had chosen David as king because of his heart. David had learned to pray long before he became king. He had learned to articulate his inner feelings, his fears, desires, regrets, and expectations. He had learned to verbalize something of the greatness of his God. Many of David's prayers have been preserved and serve as models for our worship. At least half of the psalms are ascribed to David. Many were composed for public worship in times of distress, crisis, or great joy. Some were personal in nature, while others related to national concerns.

In this lesson you will study some of David's psalms in order to learn more about your own personal worship. The lesson guides you through the following process, a process that you can use in studying other prayers and songs:

1. Read the psalm. You may want to read it several times, using more than one translation.
2. Determine the occasion on which the psalm was written. (For some psalms, we cannot determine the occasion.) You may determine it from clues within the psalm itself. In this study, you may be given an event or passage of Scripture to read.
3. Ask yourself how the writer may have felt. If you were in his or her place, how would you have felt?
4. Determine whether the psalm was written as a personal prayer or a national prayer.
5. Prepare a simple outline of the psalm, as follows:
   a. Divide the psalm into poetic stanzas or pairs of phrases based on the progression of thought. You may want to determine your own stanzas, or

use those in a translation of the Bible. You will be given couplet stanzas for this week's study.

    b. Write a short summary of each stanza, describing the subject of the stanza.

6. Reread the psalm. Analyze its content to determine what it teaches about God, about the writer, and about worship.

    a. List all that the psalm teaches about God, including what He does or has done, adjectives describing Him, and references to His character or to His attributes.

    b. List all that you can discover about the writer from the psalm. Include his or her activities, feelings, plans, and expectations.

    c. List what the psalm teaches about worship, including how to pray, what attitudes to have toward God, how to prepare for worship, how to verbalize facts or fears, ways to express thankfulness, and how to express expectations. Include anything in the psalm that can be used as a model in worship.

7. Reread the psalm. Look at your paragraph summaries. You may want to change some or all of them at this point. Write a short title (five words or less) for each stanza and a short title for the psalm.

8. From your work, formulate two or more suggestions for your own personal worship.

You will be studying a different psalm each day this week. Psalm 7 has been prepared as an example.

1. How do you think David felt when he wrote Psalm 7? (afraid, apprehensive, uncertain, doubtful)
2. Is this a personal psalm or a national psalm? (personal)
3. Briefly summarize each of the following stanzas:
   Verses 1-2 (need for refuge)
   Verses 3-5 (destruction for the guilty)
   Verses 6-9 (plea for God's action)
   Verses 10-13 (God's activities)
   Verses 14-16 (fate of the wicked)
   Verse 17 (thanks to God)
4. What does the psalm teach us about the following:
   a. God
      (righteous—v. 9)
      (searches the heart—v. 9)
      (makes the righteous secure—v. 9)
      (shield—v. 10)
      (saves—v. 10)
      (God of wrath—v. 11)
      (righteous judge—v. 11)
   b. The writer

(being pursued—v. 1)
(frightened; in danger—vs. 1-2)
(person of integrity—v. 8)
(righteous—v. 8)
(has knowledge of God—vs. 9-13)
(praises God—v. 17)
c. Worship
(relates God's past works for him—vs. 1, 10)
(verbalizes personal fears and feelings—v. 2)
(states how God acts—vs. 12-13)
(thanks God for His character and supremacy—v. 17)
5. Look at your summaries. Write brief paragraph titles and assign a title to this psalm. Use the following form:

Just Deserts

God my refuge	God's decision	God's intervention	God's work	Fate of evildoers	Benediction
Vs. 1-2	Vs. 3-5	Vs. 6-9	Vs. 10-13	Vs. 14-16	V. 17

6. Formulate two or more suggestions for worship:
   a. Articulate God's past works, particularly when threatened.
   b. Clearly state expectations, based on knowledge of God, personal spiritual state.
   c. Thank God for His answer.

DAY 1

1. Psalm 27 was written before David was anointed. Read the psalm quickly. Then read it again, more slowly, perhaps from a second translation. You may want to read it aloud.

a. Is the psalm personal or national?

b. Briefly summarize each of the following stanzas:

Verses 1-3

109

Verses 4-6

Verses 7-12

Verses 13-14

---

2. What can you learn about each of the following from Psalm 27?

God

The writer

Worship

3. Read Psalm 27 again. Look at your stanza summaries. Make any changes that seem appropriate. Write a title (no more than five words) for each stanza and one for the psalm. Place them in the following diagram:

Psalm Title:

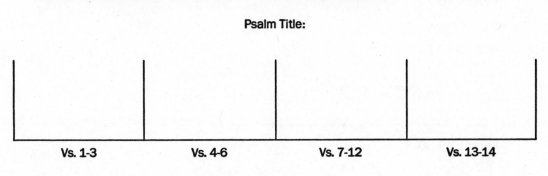

Vs. 1-3	Vs. 4-6	Vs. 7-12	Vs. 13-14

4. What are two suggestions for worship that you can find in Psalm 27?

DAY 2

5. David wrote Psalm 18 when God delivered him from Saul.

a. What do you believe his feelings were at that time?

b. Is the psalm national or personal?

c. Write a summary for each of the following stanzas:

Verses 1-3

111

Verses 4-15

Verses 16-19

Verses 20-24

Verses 25-29

Verses 30-36

Verses 37-45

Verses 46-50

---

6. What can you find out about each of the following from Psalm 18?

God

The writer

7. Read Psalm 18 again. Look at your stanza summaries as you read the psalm. Make any changes in your summaries that seem appropriate. Assign a title to each stanza and a title to the psalm. Place your titles in the following diagram.

Psalm Title:

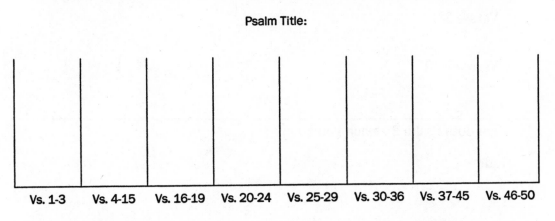

| Vs. 1-3 | Vs. 4-15 | Vs. 16-19 | Vs. 20-24 | Vs. 25-29 | Vs. 30-36 | Vs. 37-45 | Vs. 46-50 |

8. What two suggestions for worship can you make because of your study of Psalm 18?

DAY 3

9. Psalm 24 was written in the context of 1 Chronicles 15:25-16:4.

a. Read the passage. What event prompted David to write Psalm 24?

b. How do you think David felt at the time?

c. Is Psalm 24 personal or national?

d. Write a brief summary for each of the following stanzas:

Verses 1-2

Verses 3-6

Verses 7-10

---

10. What does Psalm 24 teach you about

God?

the writer?

worship?

11. Read Psalm 24 again. Make any appropriate changes in your summaries. Write a brief title for each paragraph and a title for the psalm and place them in the following diagram:

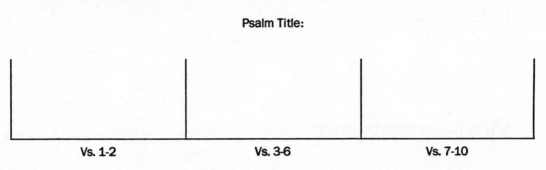

Psalm Title:

Vs. 1-2   Vs. 3-6   Vs. 7-10

12. What two suggestions for worship can you make because of your study of Psalm 24?

BONUS QUESTION
Study Psalms 20 and 21 as a unit. Psalm 20 was written before battle; Psalm 21, after battle. You may want to contrast the emotions of the writer in the two psalms in addition to using the techniques given at the beginning of this lesson.

13. David wrote Psalm 51 after the events recorded in 2 Samuel 12:1-20.

    a. What were these events?

    b. How do you think David felt?

14. a. Is Psalm 51 personal or national?

    b. Write a brief summary for each of the following stanzas:

    Verses 1-2

    Verses 3-6

    Verses 7-9

    Verses 10-12

    Verses 13-17

    Verses 18-19

15. What does Psalm 51 teach you about

God?

the writer?

worship?

16. Read Psalm 51 again. Make any appropriate changes in your paragraph summaries. Write a brief title for each paragraph and a title for the psalm. Place them in the following diagram:

Psalm Title:

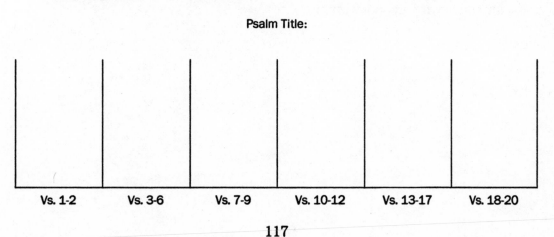

| Vs. 1-2 | Vs. 3-6 | Vs. 7-9 | Vs. 10-12 | Vs. 13-17 | Vs. 18-20 |

17. What two suggestions for worship can you make because of your study of Psalm 51?

DAY 5

18. a. Look at the psalms you studied this week. Which of them do you find most meaningful?

    b. Why?

19. a. Look at your suggestions for worship at the conclusion of each psalm study. Of your suggestions, list the three that you consider the most appropriate for your own personal worship.

b. How can you incorporate these into your personal worship in the coming week?

YOUR QUESTIONS

Why Are Healthy Friendships Important?

Life of Solomon: 1 Kings 1-11, 2 Chronicles 1-9

Under David's leadership, Israel's borders expanded farther than ever before. Solomon reaped the benefit of David's continual war with a reign of peace. Peace meant that Solomon could devote his energies to other areas, such as study, writing, building, and organizing.

DAY 1

1. Solomon succeeded David as king of Israel. Read 2 Samuel 12:1-25.

   a. Who were his parents?

   b. Why do you think he was particularly loved by David?

2. a. From 1 Chronicles 22:1-16 and 28:9-10, who chose Solomon to succeed David?

b. What specific major task did David charge Solomon to complete?

c. What additional suggestions for living did David give to Solomon?

---

3. a. From 1 Kings 1, who opposed Solomon's right to the throne?

b. Who sided with Solomon's opponent?

c. Who sided with Solomon?

d. How was Adonijah's attempt thwarted?

e. What do we learn about Adonijah's intentions from 1 Kings 2:13-25?

f. How did Solomon finally deal with Adonijah?

4. We usually think of Solomon as living a life in total obedience to God during his early years as king.

   a. From 1 Kings 3:1-15, what did he do that was contrary to God's law?

   b. How did he please God?

   c. What did God promise Solomon?

      Verses 12-13

      Verse 14

   d. How was the last promise conditional (verse 14)?

DAY 2

5. How was Solomon's wisdom evident to others?

   1 Kings 3:16-28

1 Kings 4:29-34

1 Kings 10:1-13

6. How was King Solomon's wealth described in 2 Chronicles 1:14-17 and 9:22-28?

7. During the first twenty years of his reign, Solomon built the Temple and his own palace. Read 1 Kings 6:1-7:12, and compare the two structures by completing the following chart.[1]

	TEMPLE	PALACE

Size:
  length
 	
  width
 	
  height		

Materials used		
Quality of materials		

	TEMPLE	PALACE
Time required for building		

DAY 3

8. Second Chronicles 5:1-7:10 describes the great festival which took place at the completion of the Temple.

a. List the events of that festival.

5:1

5:2-5

5:6

5:7-10

5:11

5:12-13

5:13-14

6:14-42

7:1

7:3

7:4

b. Review these events, imagining what it would be like to be present. Describe your feelings.

c. Which of these events would you have found the most meaningful?

Why?

d. How do you think Solomon felt during these events?

9. a. Read 2 Chronicles 6:14-42. What is the occasion?

b. What did Solomon ask from God?

c. What characteristics did Solomon ascribe to God?

d. According to 2 Chronicles 7:1-3, how did God respond to Solomon's prayer?

DAY 4

10. God had appeared to Solomon early in his reign, and then again after the dedication of the Temple.

a. Compare the two appearances.

	FIRST APPEARANCE (1 Kings 3:4-14)	SECOND APPEARANCE (1 Kings 9:1-9)
What was Solomon doing preceding God's appearance to him?		
What unconditional promises did God make to Solomon?		

	FIRST APPEARANCE (1 Kings 3:4-14)	SECOND APPEARANCE (1 Kings 9:1-9)
What promises depended on Solomon's obedience?		

b. How did God warn Solomon at the second appearance?

11. a. Review the first ten questions of this lesson. How was Solomon a good king?

b. What desirable traits did he demonstrate?

c. From Deuteronomy 7:1-5, 17:16-20, and 1 Kings 10:14-11:8, how did Solomon fail to obey God?

d. How did God say He would punish Solomon (1 Kings 11:9-13, 26-40)?

12. a. According to 1 Kings 11:4, what factor played a major part in Solomon's sinfulness?

b. How do you think this happened?

13. a. Who are your most intimate friends? (Name at least two.)

b. What qualities do you think you should look for in an intimate friend?

c. How are these qualities demonstrated in your most intimate friends?

d. What changes, if any, should you make in your friendships?

e. Which of your friendships would you like to cultivate?

YOUR QUESTIONS

NOTE:
1. JoAnn J. Cairns, *God's Plan for the World* (Wheaton, Ill.: Lifeway, 1982), page 60.

How Does a Leader Shape a Nation?—Part 1

1 Kings 11:26-14:18, 2 Kings 17:1-41,
2 Chronicles 13:1-20

God promised Solomon that, if he obeyed God's commands, his throne would be established forever. Solomon's wives, however, led him away from God and into idolatry. And God told Solomon that his kingdom would be divided and only one of the twelve tribes would honor his son, Rehoboam, as its king.

DAY 1

1. The fate of Solomon's kingdom is described in 1 Kings 12:1-24.

   a. What issue divided the nation?

   b. Who were the new kings after the division of the nation?

   Northern Kingdom (Israel)

   Southern Kingdom (Judah)

   c. What right did Rehoboam have to be king?

d. What mistakes did he make?

BONUS QUESTION
You are a foreign correspondent for the *Jaffa Street Journal*. Prepare a brief
report (just a few sentences) of the events in this passage and your predictions
for their effect on the economic stability of the country.

---

2. When Solomon's kingdom was divided into Israel and Judah, Jeroboam the
   son of Nebat became the first king of Israel.

   a. What qualifications for leadership do you see in him in 1 Kings 11:26-40?

   b. What did God promise Jeroboam as a reward for obedience (verses 37-38)?

3. Jeroboam's reign is described in 1 Kings 12:25-14:20.

   a. Read this passage, and list all of the things Jeroboam did that were contrary to God's laws.

   b. As a result of his sins, what did God tell Jeroboam would happen

      to him?

      to Jeroboam's family?

      to Jeroboam's descendants?

      to Israel?

4. Even though Jeroboam chose to worship idols, God gave him special demon-
strations of His superiority.

a. Complete the following chart.

SCRIPTURE	SCENE	SIGN	JEROBOAM'S REACTION
1 Kings 13:1-6,33	*God's prophet cried out against altar at Bethel, and Jeroboam ordered the prophet to be seized.*	First (v. 4) *Jeroboam's hand shriveled up.*	*Begged for restoration.*
		Second (v. 5)	*Did not change his ways.*
		Third (v. 6)	*Did not change his ways.*
1 Kings 14:1-18			*No evidence of repentance.*

b. Why do you think God gave Jeroboam these signs?

c. What do you think Jeroboam's behavior says about his concept of God?

134

5. a. Read 2 Chronicles 13:1-20. Why was Abijah's army able to defeat an army that was twice its size?

b. What faults of Jeroboam did Abijah cite?

Verses 6-7

Verse 8

Verse 9

Verse 11

c. How did God punish Jeroboam and Israel?

Verses 15-16

Verse 17

Verse 18

Verse 19

Verse 20

---

6. The Northern Kingdom, Israel, lasted 200 years (from 931 to 732 BC) The kings of Israel, together with the approximate dates they began to reign and other pertinent information, are summarized in the following chart.[1] What conclusions can you draw from this chart

about Jeroboam's spiritual influence on his contemporaries?

about Jeroboam's spiritual influence on those who followed him?

about the number of generations in the life of a dynasty?

about how the kings of Israel died?

THE KINGS OF ISRAEL

DATE	KING	LENGTH OF REIGN	RELATIONSHIP TO PREVIOUS KING	GOOD OR EVIL	RELIGIOUS PRACTICES	IMPORTANT EVENTS OF HIS REIGN	MEANS OF DEATH
931	Jeroboam	22 years	none	evil	set up golden calves at Dan and Bethel; built shrines	took ten tribes from Rehoboam; rejected the prophet from Judah	natural causes
910	Nadab	2 years	son	evil	continued the practices of Jeroboam		assassinated
909	Baasha	24 years	none	evil	continued the practices of Jeroboam		natural causes
886	Elah	2 years	son	evil	became like the house of Jeroboam; idolatry		assassinated
885	Zimri	7 days	none	evil	continued the practices of Jeroboam	killed off all of Baasha's family	suicide
885	Omri	12 years	none	evil	continued the practices of Jeroboam	built the city of Samaria	natural causes
874	Ahab	22 years	son	evil	continued the practices of Jeroboam; built temple of Baal and worshiped in it; did more to provoke God than any of his predecessors	married Jezebel; rebuilt Jericho; three years of drought; defeat and death of prophets of Baal; battle with Benhadad; Naboth's vineyard	killed in battle
853	Ahaziah	2 years	son	evil	followed the sins of Jeroboam; worshiped Baal; consulted false gods		from a fall—judgment from God
852	Joram	12 years	brother or half-brother	evil	continued the practices of Jeroboam	miraculous supply of water in ditches; Elisha's miracles	murdered
841	Jehu	28 years	none	evil	continued the sins of Jeroboam	killed Jezebel and all Ahab's descendants; killed ministers of Baal	natural causes
814	Jehoahaz	17 years	son	evil	continued the practices of Jeroboam		natural causes
798	Jehoash (Joash)	16 years	son	evil	continued the practices of Jeroboam		natural causes
782	Jeroboam II	41 years	son	evil	continued the practices of Jeroboam; restored boundaries of Israel	natural causes	
753	Zechariah	6 months	son	evil	continued the practices of Jeroboam		assassinated
752	Shallum	1 month	none	evil	(not stated)		assassinated
752	Menahem	10 years	none	evil	continued the sins of Jeroboam		natural causes
742	Pekahiah	2 years	son	evil	continued the sins of Jeroboam		assassinated
740	Pekah	9 years	none	evil		continued the sins of Jeroboam	assassinated
732	Hoshea	11 years	none	evil	(not stated)	nation taken captive by Assyria	not stated—probably died in prison

7. We will be studying more of Israel's kings in our next assignment. For now, read about the final days of the Northern Kingdom in 2 Kings 17:1-41.

   a. List the sins of which the Israelites were accused.

   b. How did God punish the last king?

   c. How did God punish the nation?

   d. Where did God place the blame for Israel's sin (verse 21)?

   e. What became of Samaria, the capital of the Northern Kingdom?

DAY 5

8. Study the "Religious Practices" column in the previous chart.

   a. Why do you think the behavior of a leader is important, based on Israel's history?

b. Why do you think God was so severe with the prophet from Judah (I Kings 13:1-32)?

9. Jeroboam's sins may be organized as follows:

Idolatrous—worshiped idols.
Disregarded the Law
Established a secular priesthood.
Failed to trust God.
Refused to listen to God's messengers.

a. How have you seen poor or evil leadership affect society?

b. In what ways might you have a negative influence on others?

c. What can you do to begin to be a better influence?

YOUR QUESTIONS

NOTE:
1. JoAnn J. Cairns, *God's Plan for the World*, teacher's guide (Wheaton, Ill.: Lifeway, 1982), page 82.

How Does a Leader Shape a Nation?—Part 2

*1 Kings 16:29-22:40; 2 Kings 8:16-10:35,
14:23-29; Amos*

DAY 1

1. Read 1 Kings 16:29-33 and 21:25-26.

a. How did Ahab become king?

b. What adjectives or phrases are used to describe him?

c. What sins did he commit?

d. Who urged him to sin?

2. Study Ahab's behavior as reported in 1 Kings 21:1-16.

a. What sins did Ahab commit?

b. What personality traits did he demonstrate?

c. What did God say would become of Ahab and his family because of Ahab's sin (1 Kings 21:21-24)?

d. How did God soften Ahab's punishment when he demonstrated sorrow (1 Kings 21:27-29)?

DAY 2

God spoke to Ahab on a number of occasions; at times He performed miracles for Ahab while at other times He sent special directions or messages through prophets.

3. Briefly summarize Ahab's reactions to the miracles and messages in the following chart.

MIRACLE OR MESSAGE	AHAB'S REACTION
1 Kings 17:1-6, 18:1-15 *No rain for three years at Elijah's word.*	
1 Kings 18:16-40 *Fire fell from heaven to consume Elijah's sacrifice.*	

142

MIRACLE OR MESSAGE	AHAB'S REACTION
1 Kings 18:41-19:2 *Heavy rain fell when Elijah prayed.*	
1 Kings 20:1-34 *Ahab to defeat army of Aram.*	
1 Kings 20:35-43 *Ahab's life to be required for that of Ben-Hadad when Ahab let him go free.*	
1 Kings 21:1-29 *Sentence pronounced on Ahab and his offspring by Elijah.*	
1 Kings 22:1-40 *Ahab to be killed in battle if he chose to go up to Ramoth Gilead.*	

4. a. Read 1 Kings 22:29-40. How did Ahab die?

b. What did he accomplish during his reign as king (verse 39)?

143

5. a. Who was Jezebel (1 Kings 16:31)?

b. Why do you think Ahab married her?

c. How did she demonstrate that she was evil?

1 Kings 18:4

1 Kings 18:19

1 Kings 19:1-2

1 Kings 21:5-15

d. How did she influence the Southern Kingdom (2 Kings 8:16-18)?

e. Jezebel outlived Ahab by fourteen years. How did she die (2 Kings 9:30-37)?

6. Jehu became king less than a generation after Ahab's death as described in 2 Kings 9:1-10:35.

a. What was Jehu's vocation (9:4-5)?

b. Who chose him to be king?

c. What was he commanded to do (9:7)?

7. a. List Jehu's activities from 2 Kings 9:1-10:28.

9:11-13

9:14-24

9:25-26

9:27-28

9:30-37

10:1-12,17

10:13-14

10:15-28

b. How did God reward Jehu (10:30)?

---

8. a. In what ways did Jehu displease God (2 Kings 10:29,31)?

b. How did Israel suffer for her sin (1 Kings 10:32)?

DAY 4

---

9. Jehu and his descendants reigned for a total of eighty-nine years, the longest time any single family ruled the Northern Kingdom. His great-grandson was Jeroboam II. Read 2 Kings 14:23-29.

a. What did he accomplish during his reign?

b. How did God use him?

c. What sins did he commit?

10. Amos, from the Southern Kingdom, was sent to prophesy against Israel in Jeroboam's day. Complete the following chart.

SCRIPTURE	SINS
Amos 2:6-8	
Amos 2:12	
Amos 5:10-13	

11. What did Amos predict would happen to Jeroboam's kingdom?

Amos 2:13-16

Amos 3:14-15

Amos 5:16-17

_____

12. Read Amos 7:10-17. As you read, keep in mind that Amaziah was not a Levitical priest, but a pagan priest and mouthpiece for Jeroboam II.

a. What was Jeroboam's reaction to Amos's prophecy?

b. What did Amos say about Jeroboam's future?

BONUS QUESTION
In what ways were Jeroboam (son of Nebat), Jeroboam II, and Ahab alike?

13. Review lesson 16 and questions 1-12 of this lesson.

    a. What effect did the kings of Israel have on their subjects?

    b. How did the nation suffer because of their poor example?

    c. How did God punish the evil kings?

14. Review the sins of Israel in the time of Jeroboam II (questions 10-12).

    a. Which of these sins are prevalent today?

    b. Underline those that are a temptation to you.

c. What can you do to avoid practicing those sins?

YOUR QUESTIONS

How Does a Leader Shape a Nation?—Part 3

Selected portions of 1 Kings, 2 Kings, 2 Chronicles 10-36

Judah, the Southern Kingdom, continued for more than a century after the dispersion of the ten northern tribes. The following chart lists the kings of Judah, lengths of their reigns, and the corresponding kings of Israel.

LENGTH OF REIGN	NAME OF KING	CORRESPONDING KING(S) OF ISRAEL
17 years	Rehoboam	Jeroboam
3 years	Abijah	
41 years	Asa	Nadab Baasha Elah Zimri Omri
25 years	Jehoshaphat	Ahab Ahaziah Joram
8 years	Jehoram	
1 year	Ahaziah	
6 years	Athaliah (queen)	Jehu
40 years	Joash	Jehoahaz Jehoash
29 years	Amaziah	Jeroboam II
52 years	Azariah (Uzziah)	Zechariah Shallum Menahem Pekahiah Pekah
16 years	Jotham	
16 years	Ahaz	Hoshea
29 years	Hezekiah	

LENGTH OF REIGN	NAME OF KING	CORRESPONDING KING(S) OF ISRAEL
55 years	Manasseh	
2 years	Amon	
31 years	Josiah	
3 months	Jehoahaz	
11 years	Jehoiakim	
3 months	Jehoiachin	
11 years	Zedekiah	

DAY 1

1. Judah had a mixture of kings—those who obeyed God and those who worshiped idols and mistreated the prophets. The relationship of each king with God had a profound effect on the nation. The good kings of the Southern Kingdom are listed in the following chart. Read each scripture passage and complete the chart.

KING AND SCRIPTURE	EVIDENCE OF LOVE FOR GOD	INDICATIONS OF SUCCESS	RESPONSE OF PEOPLE
Jehoshaphat 1 Kings 22:41-50, 2 Chronicles 17:1-10	*Sought God, removed idols and high places, had the people learn the Law.*	*Kingdom established. Fear of God in surrounding nations. Increasing power.*	*(Not stated)*
Jotham 2 Chronicles 27:1-9			
Hezekiah 2 Chronicles 29:1-11, 31:20-21, 32:1-33			

KING AND SCRIPTURE	EVIDENCE OF LOVE FOR GOD	INDICATIONS OF SUCCESS	RESPONSE OF PEOPLE
Josiah 2 Chronicles 34:1-33, 35:1-27			

2. The most prominent evil kings were Rehoboam, Ahaz, and Zedekiah. Read about each of their reigns and complete the chart.

KING AND SCRIPTURE	DEMONSTRATION OF EVIL	CONSEQUENCES	
		FOR KING	FOR PEOPLE
Rehoboam 2 Chronicles 12:1-16	*Abandoned God's laws.*	*Continual war, subjection to Egypt, loss of palace treasure.*	*Subjection to Egypt, loss of Temple treasures.*
Ahaz 2 Chronicles 28:1-27			
Zedekiah 2 Kings 24:18-25:7, 2 Chronicles 36:11-20			

3. Some of the kings began their reigns by serving God but later turned to idols or were wicked in their early years but turned to God in their later years. Study their lives and complete the following chart. Some spaces will be left blank.

KING AND SCRIPTURE	GOOD OR EVIL	DEMONSTRA-TION OF LOVE FOR GOD	INDICATIONS OF SUCCESS	HOW HE SHOWED HE WAS EVIL	INDICATIONS OF FAILURE	APPARENT REASONS FOR CHANGE
Asa 2 Chronicles 14:2-15:19	Good	Removed idols, commanded nation to serve God.	Cities built up, peace, altar of the Lord repaired.			
2 Chronicles 16:1-13	Evil			Relied on heathens rather than God for victory, imprisoned prophet, oppressed people.	Continual war.	Baasha's blockade to prevent travel between Israel and Judah.
Joash 2 Chronicles 24:1-16						
2 Chronicles 24:17-27						

KING AND SCRIPTURE	GOOD OR EVIL	DEMONSTRA-TION OF LOVE FOR GOD	INDICATIONS OF SUCCESS	HOW HE SHOWED HE WAS EVIL	INDICATIONS OF FAILURE	APPARENT REASONS FOR CHANGE
Uzziah 2 Chronicles 26:1-15						
2 Chronicles 26:16-23						
Manasseh 2 Chronicles 33:1-11						
2 Chronicles 33:12-19						

4. a. From your charts in questions 1-3, summarize the ways that kings demonstrated their love for God.

b. How did kings demonstrate that they were evil?

c. What relationship do you see between the accomplishments or failures of kings and their relationships with God?

d. From question 3, what factors influenced kings to change from good to evil?

e. How was Manasseh influenced to change from evil to good?

f. What effect did Manasseh's behavior have on the people?

5. Jehoshaphat was the son and successor of King Asa and a contemporary of Ahab. Read 1 Kings 22:41-50 and 2 Chronicles 17:1-20:34.

a. From 2 Chronicles 18, what mistakes did Jehoshaphat make?

b. How did he show his trust in God?

6. Read 2 Chronicles 20. What did Jehoshaphat do when he was threatened?

Verse 3

Verses 5-12

Verses 14-17

Verses 18-19

Verse 20

Verse 21

7. a. What were the people doing when God gave Jehoshaphat victory?

b. What implications might this have for us today?

c. What followed this miraculous defeat of Judah's enemies?

Verse 25

Verse 26

Verses 27-28

Verse 29

Verse 30

d. How did the people respond (verse 33)?

BONUS QUESTION
Prepare a television announcement about the activity in verses 22-23. Limit your announcement to three or four sentences, and begin with, "We interrupt this program to bring you this special announcement."

8. Read 2 Kings 25:1-26 and 2 Chronicles 36:11-21.

   a. How was Judah punished for her sin?

   b. What do you think the destruction of the Temple and of the walls of Jerusalem meant to the Jews?

9. a. Review the sins of the kings of the Southern Kingdom. List each sin under one or more of the following headings:

   Sins against God

   Sins against holy items (such as the Temple)

   Sins against God's messengers

   Sins against the people

Other

b. Underline those sins that you see in leaders of your nation today.

10. What did the kings of the Southern Kingdom do to help the people economically?

spiritually?

11. a. How did the sins of the kings affect their nations?

b. How did the righteous behavior of the kings affect their nations?

12. a. The kings of Judah, like those of Israel, strongly influenced the nation. Review the evidences of evil and righteousness in their lives. Prepare a profile (or list of character qualities and practices) of a leader who shapes his or her nation for good. You may include both desirable traits and practices to cultivate and undesirable ones to avoid.

b. Name one way that you think God would have you change to conform more to your profile.

c. What can you do in the coming week toward making that change?

YOUR QUESTIONS

How Does a Leader Shape a Nation?—Part 4

*Selected portions from 1 Kings,
2 Kings, 2 Chronicles*

All of the leaders of the Northern Kingdom were evil, and the nation as a whole followed their example. While the Southern Kingdom had many evil kings and periods of time when the nation was evil, it also experienced several periods of reform. In this lesson we will be studying reforms under Asa, Joash, Hezekiah, and Josiah.

DAYS 1 and 2

1. To compare the reforms under Asa, Joash, Hezekiah, and Josiah, complete the chart.

	ASA 2 Chronicles 14:1-16:14	JOASH 2 Kings 11:1-12:21 2 Chronicles 22:10-24:27	HEZEKIAH 2 Kings 18:1-20:21 2 Chronicles 29:1-32:33	JOSIAH 2 Chronicles 34:1-35:27
Spiritual and political climate when he became king	*Idolatry: high places, sacred stones, Asherah poles, incense altars throughout the nation.*	*Baal worship with its detestable practices was common.*	*All kinds of idolatry were once again common.*	*Land filled with idolatry, male prostitution, witchcraft, divination.*

	ASA 2 Chronicles 14:1-16:14	JOASH 2 Kings 11:1-12:21 2 Chronicles 22:10-24:27	HEZEKIAH 2 Kings 18:1-20:21 2 Chronicles 29:1-32:33	JOSIAH 2 Chronicles 34:1-35:27
Individuals who supported or encouraged him in his reforms				
Reforms he made				
How God blessed him				
Mistakes he made				
Enemies of Judah during his reign				

2. a. From your chart of the kings of Judah in lesson 18, calculate the approximate number of years between the reigns of David and Asa. (Approximately forty years elapsed between the death of David and the time Rehoboam became king.)

Asa and Joash

Joash and Hezekiah

Hezekiah and Josiah

b. What does the time between the reigns of these kings tell you about the spiritual condition in which each reformer found the nation?

DAY 3

3. a. When Asa was threatened by other nations on two occasions, his responses were different. Compare the two incidents.

	FIRST THREAT 2 Chronicles 14:8—15:2	SECOND THREAT 2 Chronicles 16:1-9
Opposing nation	*Cushites*	*Israel*
Asa's response to threat		

	FIRST THREAT 2 Chronicles 14:8—15:2	SECOND THREAT 2 Chronicles 16:1-9
Result of Asa's response		
Summary of God's message to Asa		

b. How long had Asa been king when the second threat occurred (2 Chronicles 16:1)?

c. How can you account for his reaction to the second threat?

d. What evils did he commit when he was reproved (2 Chronicles 16:7-10)?

e. How did God punish him (2 Chronicles 16:11-13)?

4. a. Joash was the great-grandson of Jehoshaphat. Complete the following family line, using the Scripture given.

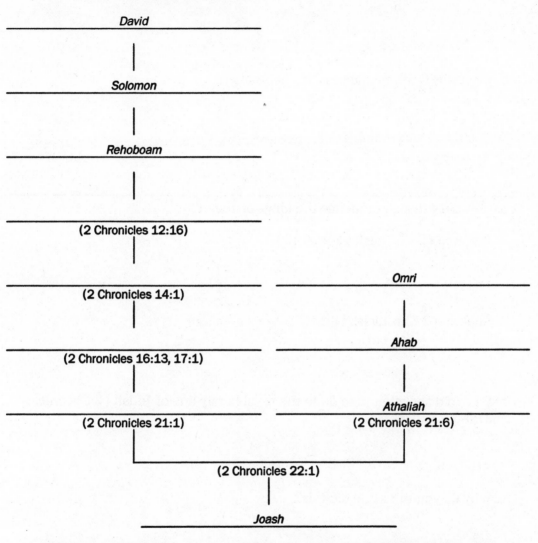

David

Solomon

Rehoboam

(2 Chronicles 12:16)

(2 Chronicles 14:1)   Omri

                                                         Ahab

(2 Chronicles 16:13, 17:1)

                                                         Athaliah
(2 Chronicles 21:1)   (2 Chronicles 21:6)

(2 Chronicles 22:1)

Joash

b. Why did Jehoshaphat encourage his son to marry Athaliah (2 Chronicles 18:1)?

c. Read 2 Chronicles 18:1-3 and 18:28-19:3. What was Jehoshaphat expected to do because of that marriage?

d. What was God's response to his behavior?

---

5. a. How did Athaliah influence the kings of Judah?

Jehoram (2 Chronicles 21:4-6,13)

Ahaziah (2 Chronicles 22:2-5)

b. What did she attempt to do to the royal family line of Judah (2 Chronicles 21:4-6, 22:10)?

c. Why do you think she did this?

d. What additional evil had she committed (2 Chronicles 24:7)?

e. What connection do you see between the ancestry of Joash and the fact that he forsook God after the death of Jehoida?

6. What miracles did God perform for Hezekiah?

   2 Kings 18:17-19:8

   2 Kings 19:9-19, 32-37

   2 Kings 20:1-11

7. Although he had been a mere child when he became king, Josiah was faithful to the Lord throughout his life.

   a. How is his devotion to the Lord described in 2 Kings 23:25?

   b. Second Chronicles 35:23-36:1 records his death. What was the response of

      the people?

      the prophet Jeremiah?

subsequent generations?

---

8. A prophet of the Lord had appeared to Jeroboam I of Israel nearly 350 years earlier with a prophecy about Josiah.

a. Study that prophecy in 1 Kings 13:1-3 and list the various elements of that prophecy.

b. Underline all the elements that were fulfilled by Josiah in 2 Kings 23:15-20.

DAY 5

---

9. a. Study your chart in question 1. What reforms did all of these kings find necessary?

b. List the mistakes of the kings and your perception of what motivated each mistake. (For example, Asa probably entered into a treaty with Benhadad because Asa had experienced wealth for so long that he feared losing the wealth more than acquiring the Lord's displeasure.)

KING	MISTAKE	POSSIBLE REASON FOR MISTAKE

170

10. a. Review questions 1-9. Make two generalizations about reform.

   b. What kind of opposition (such as social pressures or temptations) did a
      king experience?

   c. Underline any items in the list that also oppose you in your Christian walk.

11. a. From your study of the kings of Israel and Judah, prepare a list of warnings
       (at least four points) for Christians who are seeking to walk with God.

   b. Look at the items you underlined in question 10b. Which one of your warn-
      ings (listed in 11a) can apply to your life as you seek to deal with the forms
      of opposition you face?

   c. How can you apply that warning to your life in the coming week?

YOUR QUESTIONS

How Does God Speak to a Sinful Nation?

Elijah and Elisha: 1 Kings 16:1-2 Kings 13:20

At the division of Solomon's kingdom, Jeroboam became the ruler of the Northern Kingdom. Afraid that his subjects might defect to the South when they went to Jerusalem to worship, Jeroboam instituted a system of worship patterned after the idolatrous practices of the surrounding nations. Most of the people embraced the new religious system; the rest resettled in the Southern Kingdom. The majority of the people soon forgot God, but God did not forget the people. He sent prophets like Elijah and Elisha to warn and to teach them.

DAY 1

1. A prophet was responsible to proclaim God's Word to the people; he explained God's instructions and declared God's intentions for the future. Elijah's first recorded appearance was to Ahab in 1 Kings 17:1.

   a. Read 1 Kings 17:1-18:17. What was Elijah's initial message to Ahab?

   b. How do you think Ahab reacted to this appearance by an "unknown"?

   c. How was Ahab responding three years later (1 Kings 18:1-17)?

2. a. Read about Elijah's victory over the prophets of Baal and his flight from Jezebel in 1 Kings 18:18-19:21. Compare Elijah's feelings (as you view them) on Mount Carmel with his feelings when he fled from Jezebel.

DURING THE CONFRONTATION	WHEN HE FLED

b. Make a list of all that God did for Elijah in chapter 19.

c. How did God use Elijah after this incident?

1 Kings 21:1-29

2 Kings 1:1-17

3. What can we discover about Elisha from 1 Kings 19:16-21 and 2 Kings 2:1-12?

4. a. Who ruled Israel during the days of Elijah and Elisha?

Elijah:
1 Kings 17:1

2 Kings 1:1-3, 16-17

Elisha:
2 Kings 1:17

2 Kings 9:2-3

2 Kings 13:1

2 Kings 13:10

b. What was the religious atmosphere in Israel then?

DAY 3

5. The ministries of Elijah and Elisha were characterized by miracles. These miracles served a variety of purposes:

a. to punish or pronounce judgment upon a sinful person;
b. to meet a specific need of a person, such as providing food;
c. to show God's superiority and power;
d. to display God's truth.

Read about Elijah's miracles and complete the following chart.

SCRIPTURE	SUMMARY OF MIRACLE
1 Kings 17:1-6	
1 Kings 17:7-16	
1 Kings 17:17-24	
1 Kings 18:1-40	
1 Kings 18:41-45	
1 Kings 18:46	
2 Kings 2:1-8	

6. Briefly summarize Elisha's miracles in the following chart.

SCRIPTURE	SUMMARY OF MIRACLE
2 Kings 2:19-22	
2 Kings 3:1-27	
2 Kings 4:1-7	
2 Kings 4:8-17	
2 Kings 4:18-37	
2 Kings 4:38-41	
2 Kings 4:42-44	
2 Kings 5:1-18	

SCRIPTURE	SUMMARY OF MIRACLE
2 Kings 6:1-7	
2 Kings 6:8-23	

7. The miracles described in 2 Kings 1:1-17, 2:23-25, and 5:19-27 deserve special attention.

a. What do these miracles have in common?

b. What do you think God's purpose was in each of these miracles?

2 Kings 1:1-17

2 Kings 2:23-25

2 Kings 5:19-27

c. What do you think these miracles can teach us?

8. Study your charts in questions 5 and 6. Organize the miracles according to the following categories:

Miracles defying physical laws such as gravity

Miracles affecting nature

Miracles controlling health

Miracles defying death

Other

9. a. How would you describe Elijah and Elisha? (List at least four words or phrases that describe their personalities, their spiritual commitment, or their relationship to one another.)

b. How did Elijah's and Elisha's activities minister to the people of Israel?

10. a. Why do you think God used so many miracles at this time in history?

b. How would you summarize the basic message Elijah and Elisha gave to Israel?

11. a. In what ways is your society similar to that of Elijah and Elisha?

b. How is it different?

c. Summarize three truths from Elijah's and Elisha's ministry that you believe
   your society should hear.

d. What can you do to help your society hear that truth?

e. How will you do that during the next week?

YOUR QUESTIONS

LESSON TWENTY-ONE

How Can God Use Me?

*Selected scripture passages from the period
of the Divided Kingdom*

Up to this point in our study of the Divided Kingdom, we have focused on the lives of great people, famous individuals. Most of them were kings or prophets. Some were wicked, others were good. Now we will turn our attention to some of the lesser-known individuals from this period, men and women who had a major impact on their generation.

DAY 1

1. a. Read 1 Kings 17:7-24. How did this woman serve Elijah?

b. Why do you think Elijah's request might have seemed strange to the woman?

c. How was she rewarded for her service?

d. If she had refused Elijah's request, what do you think would have happened to her?

to Elijah?

---

2. a. Read 1 Kings 18:1-15. What was Obadiah's vocation?

b. What can you learn about Obadiah?

His vocation

His character

His service to God

His feelings

3. a. Read 1 Kings 22:1-28. What was Micaiah's vocation?

   b. What message did he deliver?

   c. List the people who supported Micaiah.

   d. List the people who opposed or disagreed with him.

   e. How do you think you would have felt if you were in his place?

   f. Why do you think he was able to be so bold?

   g. What happened to Micaiah because of his faithful service?

4. a. Read 2 Kings 4:8-36. What can we discover about this woman from verses 8-16?

b. Describe the room she built for Elisha.

c. How was she rewarded for her hospitality?

d. What additional aid did Elisha give her (2 Kings 8:1-6)?

DAY 3

5. a. Read 2 Kings 5:1-27. What can we find out about the Israelite girl from verses 2-3?

b. What do you think Naaman learned through this experience?

6. a. We learn how four lepers served an entire city in 2 Kings 6:24-7:20. How were these men serving God when they served the city?

b. According to Leviticus 13:45-46, how was the life of a leper (in some translations, "a man having an infectious skin disease") different from that of a non-leper?

c. How did these four lepers serve the people?

d. Why might this service have been difficult?

DAY 4

7. Jehosheba and her husband Johoiada, the priest of God, hid the infant Joash when his grandmother murdered the rest of the royal family. Read about Jehoiada's life in 2 Kings 11:1-12:16 and 2 Chronicles 24:1-6.

   a. List the steps Jehoiada planned and executed to make Joash king.

   2 Kings 11:4

   2 Kings 11:5-11

   2 Kings 11:12

2 Kings 11:13-16

2 Kings 11:17

2 Kings 11:18

2 Kings 11:19

b. What else did Jehoiada do?

2 Chronicles 24:3

2 Chronicles 24:14

2 Kings 12:2

8. a. Look at the lives of the seven individuals you have studied this week and complete the following chart. (You may leave some spaces blank.)

INDIVIDUAL	STATUS IN SOCIETY	TYPE OF SERVICE TO GOD	RISKS OR COSTS	PROFIT (IF ANY)
Woman of Zarephath in Sidon	Low	Provided food for God's prophet.	No food for herself or her son; starvation	Food miraculously lasted. Son raised from the dead.
Obadiah	High			
Micaiah	Average			
Shunammite woman	Average			
Slave girl	Very low			
Four lepers	Lowest			
Jehoiada	High			

b. From your chart, what conclusions can you make about the kind of person God uses?

YOUR QUESTIONS

How Should I Respond
to an Ungodly Government?

2 Chronicles 36, Psalm 137, Daniel

DAY 1

1. The final kings of the Southern Kingdom are described in 2 Chronicles 36:2-14. Read about their reigns and complete the following chart.

Verses	2-4	5-8	9-10	11-14
Name of King	Jehoahaz			
Length of reign	3 months			
Nature of spiritual commitment	Did evil in the eyes of the Lord.			
Evidence of spiritual commitment	(Not stated.)			
How God punished the king	He was deported to Egypt.			

191

2. a. Read 2 Chronicles 36:15-23. What did God do to motivate the people to return to Him?

b. How did the people respond to God's works?

c. List the ways that God punished the people (verses 17-21).

d. How did God enable His people to return to Israel (verses 22-23)?

DAY 2

3. The Jews spent seventy years in Babylon. During this time, Babylon was overthrown by Persia. Read Psalm 137, a psalm written during captivity, and describe the feelings of God's people.

4. a. Read Daniel 1:1-5. For whom was the king establishing a special training program?

b. What criteria were used in choosing these men?

c. How were Daniel and his three friends different from the other Jewish trainees (verses 6-21)?

d. How do you think it might have been difficult for Daniel and his friends to be different?

e. What was the result of their faithfulness to God (verses 15-21)?

DAY 3

5. Read Daniel 2, 4, and 5 and complete the following chart.

	DANIEL 2	DANIEL 4	DANIEL 5
Revelations of the future			

193

	DANIEL 2	DANIEL 4	DANIEL 5
Men who failed to interpret dream			
Rewards given to Daniel			
What was revealed about Daniel's character			

DAY 4

6. When Daniel and his friends chose to obey God's Word rather than follow the orders of the king, they risked their positions and their lives. Study each passage of Scripture and complete the following chart.

	DANIEL 1:8-17	DANIEL 3:1-30	DANIEL 6:1-28
Men involved	*Daniel, Hananiah, Mishael, Azariah*		
What they refused to do	*Eat the king's meat.*		
Risks of their action	*Disciplinary action, dismissal, prison, execution*		

	DANIEL 1:8-17	DANIEL 3:1-30	DANIEL 6:1-28
Actions taken by their superiors	*Agreed to trial period.*		
How God helped them	*Gave them favor in eyes of official. Gave them knowledge and understanding.*		

7. a. Review questions 4-6. In what ways were these men expected to compromise their beliefs and practices?

b. In what ways might they have been punished for refusing to comply with the expectations of their superiors?

c. What would their action have cost them if they had complied with their superiors?

d. Put yourself in the place of Daniel and his friends. Of the three examples of obeying God rather than the king (question 6), which do you think would have been the most difficult for you?

DAY 5

8. a. Review questions 4-6. How do you think biblical behavior conflicts with common behavior in our world today? Name at least five specific differences.

b. What risks do you take when you refuse to follow practices accepted by your society?

c. How do you think these risks compare with the risks Daniel and his friends took?

d. How has God rewarded you when you obeyed Him?

---

9. a. What do Romans 12:2 and 1 John 2:15-16 tell us about our relationship to the world?

b. What are some of the ungodly practices or philosophies of the world that you find hard to resist?

c. Review question 7. What relationship do you see between those practices you find difficult to resist and the practices Daniel and his friends were expected to endorse?

d. How does John describe our ability to resist (1 John 2:14)?

e. How do you think understanding the experiences of Daniel and his friends can help us to choose to be faithful to God?

YOUR QUESTIONS

How Should I Respond to Opposition?

Ezra, Nehemiah, Esther, and Haggai

From the death of Joshua to the capture of the Southern Kingdom by Nebuchadnezzar, Israel was characterized by idolatry. Brief periods of reform and destruction of idols were followed by longer periods of backsliding and idol worship.

God repeatedly warned both kingdoms of coming judgment for their idolatry, but they continued their pagan practices. Finally the northern tribes were taken captive by Assyria and assimilated into its culture. Several generations later, Nebuchadnezzar attacked the Southern Kingdom; his armies destroyed the city walls and the Temple, carried off the wealth, and deported the people to Babylon.

The people mourned and longed for their homeland. Some of the royal descendants were forced to serve the king of Babylon. Then Persia conquered Babylon. Many Jews were absorbed into the Babylonian and Persian cultures and lost their Jewish identity. Finally, after seventy years, Cyrus, the king of Persia, issued a proclamation allowing all who desired to do so to return to Jerusalem to rebuild the Temple. More than eighty years were required to rebuild the Temple, houses, and the wall of Jerusalem.

DAY 1

1. Scan Ezra 1:1-6:22 and Haggai 1:1-2:9 and identify the major events described in the scripture passages in the following chart. Label each event as a positive step toward reconstruction (+) or an act of opposition to reconstruction (-).

SCRIPTURE	EVENT	+ OR -
Ezra 1:1-4	*Cyrus granted the Jews permission to return if they wanted to.*	+
Ezra 1:5, 2:64-70		

SCRIPTURE	EVENT	+ OR -
Ezra 3:1-6		
Ezra 3:10-13		
Ezra 4:1-5	*The enemies of the Jews sought to frustrate the plans to rebuild the Temple.*	+
Ezra 4:6-24		
Haggai 1:1-15, Ezra 5:1-2		
Ezra 5:3-6:13		
Ezra 6:14-22		

DAY 2

2. The Jews returned to Israel in three separate contingents. The return of the first group is recorded in Ezra 1:1-2:70.

a. Why did Cyrus allow the captives to return?

b. Which of the captives were allowed to return?

200

c. How were their financial needs met?

d. How many returned?

---

3. Compare the three returning groups by completing the following chart.

	1 Ezra 1:1-2:2, 2:64-3:13, 5:1-2, 6:13-15	2 Ezra 7:1-8:36	3 Nehemiah 1:1-29
Approximate date of return	538 BC	458 BC	444 BC
Leader(s)			
Assigned task			

---

4. What did each of the following aspects of reconstruction mean to the Jewish people?

Rebuilding the altar

Rebuilding the Temple

DAY 3

5. List the major events of the return of the second group.

SCRIPTURE	MAJOR EVENT	+ OR -
Ezra 7:1-10		
Ezra 7:11-28		
Ezra 8:15-36		

6. Quickly read about the third returning group in Nehemiah 1:1-7:3 and
12:27-47. Complete the following chart. (You could list eight to ten events.)

SCRIPTURE	EVENT	+ OR -

7. The Jewish leaders experienced opposition throughout the reconstruction. The opposition was both external (coming from outside the Jewish body) and internal (coming from within the Jewish body). Study the scripture passages and complete the following chart.

SCRIPTURE	OPPOSING PARTY	FORM OF OPPOSITION	HOW OPPOSITION WAS HANDLED	EXTERNAL OR INTERNAL
Ezra 4:1-3	*Enemies of Judah*	*Wanted to assist in rebuilding Temple.*	*Leaders refused to accept help.*	*External*
Ezra 4:4-5	*People around them*	*Tried to discourage Jews, frustrate plans.*	*Ignored.*	*External*
Ezra 4:6-6:15				
Nehemiah 4:1-6				
Nehemiah 4:7-9				
Nehemiah 4:10-23				

SCRIPTURE	OPPOSING PARTY	FORM OF OPPOSITION	HOW OPPOSITION WAS HANDLED	EXTERNAL OR INTERNAL
Nehemiah 5:1-13	*Jewish nobles*	*Exacted high taxes.*	*Confronted nobles.*	*Internal*
Nehemiah 6:1-9				
Nehemiah 6:10-13				

8. The events recorded in Esther occurred after the rebuilding of the Temple but before Nehemiah returned to Jerusalem. Quickly read the book of Esther.

    a. How did these events constitute a threat to the reconstruction?

    b. How did Mordecai deal with the situation?

9. Dedications followed the completion of the Temple and of the wall. Compare these celebrations.

	TEMPLE Ezra 6:16-22	WALL Nehemiah 12:27-43
Emotions of people		
Length of celebration		
Activities		

10. a. Review the ways in which the people experienced opposition to rebuilding. How have you faced similar opposition in your own life?

b. Select one form of opposition with which you are frequently confronted.

c. How do you most frequently handle this type of opposition?

d. How did the godly Old Testament people deal with the same type of opposition?

e. How can you apply the approach of the Old Testament characters to your own circumstances?

YOUR QUESTIONS

What Follows Revival?
Ezra, Nehemiah, Haggai, and Malachi

When Cyrus issued his decree, all Jews were given permission to return to Jerusalem. But very few of the original captives were still alive or able to make the trip. Most of the new generation considered Babylon home; they had adopted the customs and culture of Babylon and even intermarried. The first contingent that returned had a strong faith in the God of their fathers and were willing to sacrifice the comfort of Babylon for the land God had promised them.

DAY 1

1. Until Jerusalem was captured by Nebuchadnezzar and the people taken to Babylon, they repeatedly engaged in idolatry. But after the seventy-year exile, the Jews never committed idolatry again. Read Ezra 1:3, 3:1-6:22, and Haggai 1:1-2:23.

   a. How did the returning Jews feel about rebuilding the Temple when they arrived in Jerusalem?

   b. What deterrents to completing this task did they experience?

   c. What were they apparently doing at the time of Haggai's prophecy?

d. Why did Haggai rebuke them for this?

e. How prosperous were they?

f. What did Haggai command them to do?

g. How did they respond?

2. Ezra led a second group to Israel at least two generations after the return of the first group. What do we learn about Ezra's spiritual leadership from Ezra 7:1-10:34?

REFERENCE	FACTS

3. a. Read Ezra 9:1-10:17. What spiritual problems did Ezra find?

   b. Complete the following chart by stating Ezra's actions in the left column and the response the people then had to Ezra in the right column. Scripture references are given for each part of the chart.

EZRA'S ACTION	PEOPLE'S RESPONSE TO EZRA
(9:3-4)	(9:4)
(9:5-10:1)	(10:1-4)
(10:5)	(10:5)
(10:10-11)	(10:12-17)

4. Both Ezra and Nehemiah returned during the reign of Artaxerxes. Read Nehemiah 1:1-2:20. Then review questions 2 and 3 and compare Nehemiah with Ezra.

	EZRA	NEHEMIAH
Vocation		

	EZRA	NEHEMIAH
Evidences of spiritual commitment		
Effect on people		

DAY 3

5. a. Read Nehemiah 8:1-9:38. What activities made the Jews aware of their spiritual need?

b. How did the people respond to their need?

8:14-18

9:1-36

9:38

6. What did the Jewish people agree to do after this time of revival (Nehemiah 10:20-39)?

Verse 30

Verse 31

Verses 32-34

Verses 35-38

Verse 39

DAY 4

7. Nehemiah went back to Persia and resumed his responsibilities after the dedication of the wall. He made a second trip to Jerusalem several years later. Read Nehemiah 13:4-31.

a. What sins did Nehemiah find upon his return?

b. How well had the people kept the vows they had made at the time of the dedication of the wall? (Review Nehemiah 10:20-39, question 6.)

8. Sanballat and Tobiah made repeated attempts to interfere with Nehemiah and with the spiritual commitment of the people.

a. Complete the following chart.

SCRIPTURE	METHOD OF INTERFERENCE
Nehemiah 2:19	*Mocked and ridiculed the workers. Accused the Jews of rebelling against the king of Persia.*
Nehemiah 4:1-3	*Ridiculed the people and the quality of their work.*
Nehemiah 4:7-8	
Nehemiah 6:1-9	
Nehemiah 6:10-14	
Nehemiah 6:17-19	

SCRIPTURE	METHOD OF INTERFERENCE
Nehemiah 13:4-9	
Nehemiah 13:28	

b. How did Sanballat and Tobiah turn the hearts of the people away from God?

---

9. The book of Malachi was written less than fifty years after the time of Nehemiah.

a. How does Malachi describe the nation?

Malachi 1:6

Malachi 1:7-8

Malachi 2:11

Malachi 3:8

Malachi 3:13-14

b. What similiarities do you see between the people of Nehemiah's time and those of Malachi's time?

10. The Israelites experienced repeated times of revival. We might look at their spiritual condition as occurring in three stages:

- Revival; they repented of their sins and turned to God.
- Worship and service for God; they received blessings from God.
- Apostasy or return to sin; frequently they committed the same sins again.

These stages can be illustrated by the following diagram:

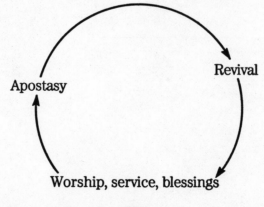

214

a. Review questions 1-9. In the following chart list the major points of revival or apostasy as you see them. Then indicate whether the incident was revival or apostasy.

EVENT	REVIVAL OR APOSTASY

b. How do you account for apostasy shortly after revival?

11. a. Review question 5. What factors caused the people to realize their need for revival?

b. How can you use the same means to continually remind yourself of your need for God?

c. Name at least three habits or tendencies that tend to draw you away from God.

d. What positive action can you take to prevent apostasy in your own life?

YOUR QUESTIONS